MAKE
IT
HAPPEN!

MAKE IT HAPPEN!

A LITTLE BLACK BOOK ON HOW TO MAKE THINGS HAPPEN

LAZAR VUKOVIC

BLAKE HOUSE
PUBLISHING

Blake House Books may be purchased for educational, business or sales promotional
use. For information please email the Special Markets Department at
SMD@BlakeHousePublishing.co.uk

FIRST EDITION

Designed by Stanislav Kruhliak

ISBN 978-1-5272-8765-5

Printed and bound by CPI Group (UK) Ltd, Croydon CR0 4YY

Be somebody. Somebody nobody else can be.

You.

CONTENTS

FOREWORD
JOHN CHALLIS

In Only Fools and Horses my friend Del Trotter has a motto: 'He Who Dares...' Well, if this handy book had been around when he started out, you can bet it would have been Del's go-to reference manual.

My friend Lazar is just your average guy, or so he would have us believe. Some of us go through life expecting things to come to us, but this young man hit the ground running!

He was a child with a vivid imagination, and his enquiring mind and determination to succeed have seen him go through the card of business ventures.

Not everything goes according to plan, but he never hangs around; it's on to the next project, no regrets.

Lazar's evident passion and dedication have taken him all over the world, and he is a true entrepreneur.

I hope this will inspire you to run with your ideas and hopes, to never give up and to be the best you can.

This time next year...

Phil Challis

FOREWORD
JAMES COLLIER

co-founder of Huel

I n the jungle of business, you may, if you're lucky, come across a certain type of creature. Members of this subspecies are extremely rare and have a certain type of mindset that can manifest itself in a variety of ways, but it always displays creativity and possesses the ability to predict likely behaviours of humans. It can morph its own behaviour in a way that will result in actions that propel any business it sets its heart on into a booming success. These creatures have a certain 'genotype', and they're not present in every successful business; I've only ever met a few of them. They are known as entrepreneurs.

I first came across Lazar Vukovic – Laz, as we call him – 12 or so years ago at a local gym where we both trained: a well-presented (even in his training attire), chatty and friendly guy who was always smiling; the sort of guy you like from the outset. Sometime later – it's hard to pinpoint precisely when – we became close friends. (It's a standing joke between Laz and I that he's my 'closest friend' as he currently resides less than a quarter of a mile from me!) In the time we've been friends, I've seen him turn his hand to a lot of things. I spotted his drive and ambition years ago, but only more recently did I notice that he was, indeed, a member of the aforementioned entrepreneur subspecies. Looking back, it was staring me in the face all along: he possessed a varied range of skills, considerable experience in varied industries, the gift of the gab, a large portfolio of contacts, lots of motivation and an incredible work ethic.

But also, and more importantly, he had the ability to spot a likely success and then immerse himself into the venture for a few weeks in order to understand the intricacies behind it, and then delegate the tasks while continuing to coordinate in a helicopter fashion. He also knows when it's time to quit if things aren't working out, whilst accepting that quitting can actually be moving forward. Laz never complains about having too much to do, he just does what needs to be done.

Make It Happen is an enjoyable insight into the workings of the mind of someone from this subspecies; it certainly shows what makes this particular entrepreneur tick. Some of the stories I already knew, but many I didn't, and even for the ones I did know, I hadn't previously been aware of Laz's mindset around them.

I attended the Lifeline gala he organised for HRH Crown Princess Katherine at Claridge's, London (page 93), with my wife. It was an incredible event, impeccably organised, and we enjoyed the evening very much. I've organised large events myself, albeit of a different type, so I can appreciate the amount of mental energy, passion and pride required in order to make them run smoothly. I hung around after the event, and I was smiling to myself in admiration of the way Laz continued to faff around even after everyone had gone home, demonstrating the amount of care he takes in what he does. Laz and I are wired up differently in many ways, and there are a number of ideologies to which he refers in Make It Happen that we don't share. But Laz and I have a lot more in common: we both enjoy business and exercise, respect family values, have the same ridiculous sense of humour and, most notably, we both like to 'make it happen'. This could be why we get on so well … but I don't think this is the main reason. It's more likely because he's a warm-hearted, friendly, nice guy whose company is enjoyable to be in.

If you're someone who wants to 'make it happen', you'll love reading this book and will certainly benefit from Laz's experiences. But you don't need to be someone who's particularly driven in business to enjoy this book; seeing how a mind like Laz's works is fascinating, and you'll enjoy the narrative of his life so far.

Laz will achieve a great deal in the world of business, and he will certainly be what most people would describe as 'a success'. But, will someone with a mind like Laz's ever feel he's 'made it'? I don't think so, and that's a good thing. A person who's as driven as Laz will always take pleasure from progressing themself further.

PART I

HOW I MADE
IT HAPPEN!

CHAPTER

1

Who are you?

Have you ever had an idea or thought about an opportunity and then done nothing and let it pass you by? I want this book to demonstrate how to Make It Happen – how to take that idea, that opportunity, that casual conversation, and turn it into something BIG!

I'm not a billionaire or a big-shot investor with a limitless supply of money that is waiting to be thrown at the next idea. I'm that person/friend/relative you know who's always up to something new and always has a story to tell. From a young age, I've strongly believed that you can 'own it all' (an idea that came from playing Monopoly). Some who know me well say that I have a tycoon mindset, which I love to hear, and I'm still waiting for that tycoon bank balance to follow! I won't tell you what the others say. After reading this book, you can say it for yourself!

2020 was probably the worst year in living history for most, a year that was lost, time stood still, everybody 'went home' and stayed home for a long time. I'm attempting to write this book as we near 2021, when I hope that we have a lot of 'old'-normal revivals and we get back to normality, whatever that means anymore.

My aim with this book is to share some of my stories of how I've made things happen – some good, some bad, some I guess just outright crazy. I hope they make you laugh out loud, inspire you and motivate you to get that idea off the ground. Failing that, I hope this book comes in useful and is able to prop the laptop up while on a Zoom call, keep that door open or keep you warm if that fire is running low on wood.

I've had a lot of people approach me for business advice. Usually, my first instinct is a childish giggle. My inner child wakes up and says, 'You've got to be kidding me – somebody asking you for advice?' Once I realise that I'm no longer that eight-year-old kid (which I'm still coming to terms with) and that I'm 35 years old, I gulp, reality sets in, and then I start talking. I've always found this part of me so fascinating, like I'm that same child, just in a grown-up body … Anyway, enough of the waffle, I want to get down to business and try to explain what it is that makes me tick, gives me motivation and makes me get out there and hustle. As you'll notice by the style of my writing, I have this split personality, one part being that eight-year-old immature kid, and the other something of an Alan Sugar, no-nonsense, to-the-point character.

I'm a big believer in the idea that you can be whatever you want to be. If you want to be an actor but would also like to be a lawyer and an inventor – why can't you be? Ever since my childhood, I've been fascinated with so many different things that I believe you can be multidisciplined in the areas you are interested in. People change careers; they change their path because they want to develop. But there's also a point where you're about to make such a big decision that it can change your future for good. These are the decisions that most people find scary, and it puts them off. They run a mile because of the risk of change that comes with it.

What I want to share is that no matter what your background, ethnic origin or personal circumstances, there is nothing standing in your way of making it happen – apart from you, of course! This book isn't a CV of achievements, but stories of experiences. Hopefully, you can take the best bits from them and apply that knowledge where you need to.

I want to share my journey with you from childhood to today in a series of stories. These are short tales of times when I spotted an opportunity, had an idea or created something out of thin air. I'm not famous or any more privileged than any other person, but over time I managed to make several things happen, all by using my intuition and putting myself in various situations. I always wanted to make big things happen, and that's what I strive for. If I can do it, so can you! I hope my stories can bring you some entertainment as well as motivation to make that idea of yours a reality.

On a personal note, I'd like to thank you for reading this book. Whatever you may think of it, please share that feedback with me. This is my first book and could well be my last, so I understand that it may not be perfect. I hope that reading it motivates you to make that idea, opportunity or passion you have into something BIG!

Yu-Go England

Without going into too much detail, I am a child to immigrants to the UK. My mother, God rest her soul, came to the UK with her family in the late sixties when she was just 12. My grandfather couldn't cut looking after cattle on a farm anymore after exploring a bit of the city, so they left what was then Yugoslavia to head to the promised land and found themselves in a rural town called Corby, with my grandfather working at British Steel. I guess for him it was more the glamour he loved; he was often known as 'The Doctor' for walking around the town dressed impeccably smart. He always wore a suit, carried his leather briefcase, and there was an air about him that signified 'importance'. He would arrive at work, get his overalls out of this leather briefcase and start doing his job, washing windows around one of Britain's largest steel plants. He was a very proud man and a ladies' man, but a larger-than-life character, with his ambitions of leaving the family home and acres of land to set sail with his wife and four children to an unknown land, to speak an unknown language all to fulfil a life which he had dreamed of. We've all heard of those stories of rags to riches or a child brought up in poverty who made millions. My grandad wasn't a millionaire in financial terms, but he was a billionaire with the heart he had. One of my main lessons in life came from my grandfather who, when was fit and well, would display that he was the pillar of the family, keeping us all together, cooking Sunday lunch and entertaining his clan. These distant memories will always last and signify the importance of keeping your family together.

Fast-forward from the sixties to '86 and my mother has just given birth to her only son. There I was in a small town in rural England known as 'Little Scotland', about to embark on an adventure even William Wallace wasn't ready for – and I'm not talking about fighting to get to the front of the queue in Iceland to get my cheap Irn-Bru either! I'm talking about growing up in a town that wasn't cosmopolitan at the time and having to deal with a dual identity, speaking a non-English language and having customs that kids would love to take the mickey out of. These customs would shine the spotlight on me being more 'different' than the other kids in the neighbourhood.

My father was 'the main man'. Now, he wasn't involved in the mafia or a serial killer (although he did resemble Peter Sutcliffe and sometimes I would joke that my father had buried an awful lot of people), but when people would meet him they would kiss his hand whether that be in the street or at the front door. Could you imagine the look on the neighbours' faces? Well, my father was (and still is) an Orthodox Priest, and kissing a priest's hand is taught as a way of respecting Christ. While all this might sound fun and jovial now, let me tell you it was a nightmare growing up with. I had to deal with a lot of piss taking and having to explain things like why I celebrate Christmas on 7th January instead of 25th December.

Similar to my grandfather, my father emigrated to the UK from Montenegro in the seventies, but he came alone and with one intention: to marry my mother. While he was studying theology and practising to become a priest, he had seen my mother's photo as part of a choir in a church magazine and started writing letters to her. She didn't reply and he carried on writing. Now after the fourth letter my grandmother inclined that my mother should reply as a matter of courtesy since he is practising to become a priest. Basically, I think she felt a bit of pity for him. Well, with that one reply from my mother, not too far down the line, my father finds himself at the front door of my grandparents' house with his twin brother, ready to ask for my mother's hand in marriage.

Now, although I haven't even yet scratched the surface of the main topic of the book, this little insight should prove helpful when referencing some of the stories I have to tell later in this book.

These little insights into the lives of my grandfather and my father have shown that they 'Made It Happen' – although not business related, the action that they took provided the result they had in mind, hence the need to make it happen.

This is the journey I want to take you on throughout the rest of the book so you can find out more about how to 'make it happen!' and apply it where you may need to in your own life.

Costa-del-Corby, it's on the map!

Anybody that knows me has heard this line a lot: Costa-del-Corby? Where is that? The UK? Spain? What? Huh? It's on the map; Corby is that small town I was telling you about, known as the home of the Scots and famous for its steel works with British Steel, now one of the UK's fastest-growing towns – and that's nothing to do with the sales of Irn-Bru! I must admit it was 'rough' growing up here as a kid. In the nineties, employment was low, crime was high – it was probably one of the worst places to live in the UK. However, as dreadful as it sounds, the majority of people in this town have been among the friendliest and caring people I've met to date, but as in most cases, a bad egg spoils the others and the bad eggs were the ones that caught the attention of the national media and generally gave the town a bad name. Well, at least that was true of the estate I grew up on. As I write about this now I reflect and think, there were no phones, no GPS/locations to send home to let your mum know where you were. You'd come home when the streetlights came on and there were a much more general sense of safety, but as a kid, you knew where to go and where not to go, as those no-go zones only meant trouble.

Growing up on the estate, my friends were from English-speaking backgrounds (English, Scottish, Irish), and all the jokes we used to tell each other would be about 'an Englishman, am Irishman and a Scotsman'. To address the elephant in the street – that would be me – coming from a background with a non-English family and my father being a man of very few words in English at the time, it could become quite embarrassing at times. For example, one summer night, playing 'footie' in the street with friends, my father shouted, 'Lazar, gay in the house!' This left my friends looking at each other puzzled, me shouting back to my father quickly in Serbian, trying to cover what he just said, as if it was Serbian he was speaking to me in, and then me casually saying goodbye to my friends before running 100mph back home in order to not hear a repeat of what he just said. (For the record he meant 'Get in the house'.) There were frequent embarrassing occasions like this in front of friends, and I'm sure anybody with a different ethnic background to their friends could recall some social awkwardness they've faced with native speakers at some point or another.

When I was growing up, there was a Serbian community in the town, albeit not very large. Well, not large enough for me to have friends my own age I could speak Serbian to on a regular occasion. This meant that as a child, my Serbian was very limited as I didn't practise it. My view was I'd only speak Serbian to my family or when within the community, which was generally to communicate with an older audience, so I grew fairly ignorant to the language, only to find out that later on in life I'd be speaking the language as much I speak English!

The Serbian community in Corby was and still is a great community. There is a Serbian Orthodox church (I'll tell you more about that later), which on reflection worked like a social network back in the day when I was a child. If you needed a plumber, accountant or you were looking for a job, you would go to a Sunday church service and find that person or introduction there. Perhaps your intention for going to church wasn't wholly for worship; the congregation that attended meant that back in the nineties it really was the place to network, as I'm sure it was for generations before the advancement of social media. Being born in the UK to parents of Serbian origin, attending church and helping my father out at services meant that I was stamped with this identity of being Serbian.

I'd use the joke of Costa-del-Corby being a tropical part of England, mainly because when I'd visit Montenegro or Serbia during the summer with temperatures hitting well over 38 degrees, many would try to tease me and say, 'Missing the rain in England?' I eventually got fed up of dealing with these sorts of comments and started to reply with, 'It's actually warmer in Costa-del-Corby' … and it's been on the map ever since!

Church boy

Being a son of a preacher meant I was in church almost as much as my father was. I would be the altar boy helping my father out, whether that meant lighting candles or lighting the charcoal for the incense – I was there, in the altar (working) from a young age. If you haven't been to an Orthodox church, the altar is concealed by a wooden structure with icons painted on it. Now, walking into church and past the worshippers to go into the altar came with a sense of privilege as you were at the 'front of the show'. It also meant that I'd be the messenger boy during services, running back and forth and passing various messages. All the tasks I carried out I did with such seriousness, I'm sure the congregation used to chuckle … or it fell in within the cold Eastern European poker face look of showing no emotions and I blended in perfectly. Whichever it was, I loved it!

I'd also be the kid that walked around the church with the collection plate. This is part of my childhood that sparked the commercial side. Imagine the feeling of being five or six years old, opening a door and seeing 50 to 100 people all rushing to their pockets as soon as they see you. You'd be the signal for everyone to look for money. I can still hear the coins jingle today. I'd start off by collecting closest to the altar, which would be my mother and the choir, then lead up to the congregation. By the end of the collection your arms would hurt as you'd be holding them out at a 90-degree angle, and don't forget the size of the coins in the nineties – they were huge! I'd collect all the money and drop it off at the entrance to the church for the treasurer, who would empty all the money into the money bag, return the collection plate to me and start counting. I'd always walk back to the altar with a sense of achievement. Although I didn't really do anything apart from walk around with a plate – I mean, I wasn't appealing person to person – I still felt that I had achieved something. This would become something that later on in life would serve a purpose – fundraising!

There would be various days throughout the year that the Serbian priests from all over the UK would get together to celebrate a patron saint, or there would be a church festivity of sorts that would be all very high-brow stuff with the bishop flying in from Sweden. It would be a chance to show off how quick you can light the candles and charcoal, and collect money with that all-important plate. Jokes aside, it almost felt like a very important club to be part of, but it also gave me a wider understanding of how an organisation worked. I'd also be present at some important meetings I think I shouldn't have been part of, mainly because I would have been in the room for so long and kept quiet (wasn't my place to say anything) and/or because perhaps they thought I didn't understand Serbian so well. Whichever it was, I think my eyes used to grow larger with more information I'd hear that I shouldn't have! If you're wondering what sort of information that could have been, it was more about the costs to keep the churches functioning. As a kid, even hearing 'one-thousand pounds' was enough for you to lose grip of your Panda Pops or Capri-Sun.

One great benefit that I'm thankful for was that belonging to the church through my family from a young age meant that I had mutual grounds with many people which would last a lifetime. Regardless of religion it's about being part of a community, club or organisation it simply puts you in touch with a lot of people over your lifetime. My father taught me to make friends wherever I go in the world as you never know when your paths might cross in life. On the other hand, an enemy is one that will always find its way to you. I cherish these wise words today.

2

Growing up

Growing up I guess I tended to get roped into quite a lot of bizarre things, such as selling a bride. What? Yes, I did sell a bride, and no it wasn't the famous 'Russian Bride', although on reflection I was 6 years old and I was playing an important part in Serbian custom at a wedding. The role is to sell the bride as part of an old Serbian custom, similar to that of a 'dowry'. It's seen as more of the entertainment point of the wedding day whereby the brother/cousin of the bride sells her to the best man and he then takes the bride to church where the groom is waiting. Now, being a six-year-old kid in the nineties, what did I turn to the night before the wedding? Yep, the Argos catalogue! I didn't have any idea how much a bride could fetch (where was the internet when I needed it?), but I thought to myself, 'Let's have a look and see what tickles my fancy.' After a good half an hour, I found it. I remember it as clear as daylight: 'Porsche Power Scalextric set' at £52.50. I marvelled at it for hours; I knew it was what I wanted. I even double-checked the 'Index' catalogue – that was as far as you'd go in price checking in those days. The decision was made!

There I was about to sell my cousin when I got called to her room before I had to walk her down the stairs to her fate. Just for clarity, it was all kosher; she wanted to marry the man in question, and they met mutually, before I get pulled up for any trade-deals against somebody's will. My cousin said, 'Well, you'd better get a lot of money.' At this point I'm sure I must have felt numb and gave a blank expression and not said anything. Well, we got ushered to get a move on, so I walked my cousin down the stairs into the living room where a Serbian accordion player was playing the traditional music you'd hear just about anywhere Serbian, and he was squeezing the poor accordion to death. My ears were ringing, I couldn't hear my own thoughts. I see the chap sitting at the table, one arm out on the table and the other on his hip (I guess it was his wallet he was keeping a hold tight of). I eventually made it to the table. What was only a few metres felt like a mile to get to, and I had a VHS camera in my face on one side and my father on the other saying the customary saying that I had to repeat in Serbian, which I sheepishly repeated, knowing that I could never tell my friends or teacher what I'd done that weekend.'

'So, how much do you want?' I heard the best man ask.

'£50,' I said. I gathered I must have had £2.50 lying around somewhere to make up for the Scalextric set I had in mind, and what do brides sell for anyway?

'More, more!' the bride belched out. As quick as John Wayne, the best man's hand moved from the hip, opened up the wallet and voila! £50 appeared in the palm of my hand.

'Done!' he said, and at that point I did feel like I was on the bad side of the deal, but I thought to myself, 'Well this is a practice run, I've got two older sisters yet to get married, I'd better study the market more!'

Bless him

As you've probably already guessed, I used to get roped into all sorts of customs and traditions. The hardest part was that you felt like you didn't have much choice. My father being the parish priest would undertake various duties around the parish, such as the annual blessing of holy water. Now, an Orthodox priest has an incense burner that they carry with them, and it would generally be a sort of small bowl with chains that had bells attached to it. Once swung around during prayers, it would remind the worshippers that their prayers are being listened to and are being lifted up. The incense burner would hold one or a few pieces of charcoal which were such a pain to light; the amount of blistered fingers I got from this thing was unreal. The incense would then sit on the charcoal and set off pleasantly smelling aromas and cause everything to be covered in a sort of white smoke. Well, my father would visit these houses to bless holy water, but he'd need someone to help him, so there I was in the passenger seat, holding the incense burner, trying not to burn my hands or my feet as we drove from house to house.

Remember the show Cribs? I would have loved to film the memories of going from house to house, exploring the interiors from forties to chic to very nineties, and meeting all the different characters at each house. It was always a similar routine at each house: greetings, small talk, prayer, 'must go'. I watched my father in awe at how good he was at communicating with people. Every household had so much respect for my father; you could say I was very, very proud.

From the 'must go' to getting in the car, many people would want to tip my father. Sometimes they'd win the mini-arm wrestle with him to put some money in his palm, or sometimes they'd put the money in my pocket. There would, however, be that one or two who would sort of say goodbye in a stand-off position with you, as if you were playing Russian roulette, twitching to see who goes first to open the door handle. Me, I loved these awkward moments, it really made me chuckle inside. I mean, these people of course wanted you round to bless holy water, but they clearly didn't want to tip, not because they couldn't, but simply because they didn't feel the need to, and I loved that! These people were from a certain geographical area which I won't disclose, but boy did I love it!

I will never forget that one year when nobody even tried to attempt to arm-wrestle my father to pass him a tip, but instead, that particular year, they all flocked to me. Was it the Brylcreem or the Paco Rabanne fragrance I was using? I don't know, but I remember having an awkward conversation with my father about a percentage split at the end of the day. After a tense moment of Eastern European bluffing I gave him 100% of it, to which he'd always 'tip' me.

My tech love

I'll never forget the first computer I used and got to love. It was 1990 and I was four years old when I first set eyes on the Amstrad 464 Plus with its built-in game, a car simulator called Burnin' Rubber. It was love at first sight! It came with a book that had pages of code to programme in 'Basic' in order to pull up a line of text for you to pretend to interact with. It was ground-breaking stuff.

It later materialised that my father had bought this computer with the intention of printing out church schedules and communicating with the parish via printed letters, notices etc. The primary reason was not for me to play games on it. I didn't mind, in fact I quickly became IT support to my father. Studying the manual that came with the computer, I was completely immersed in the cutting-edge technology of a blue screen and yellow text.

News travelled fast and I was named a 'whizz kid' one day at my primary school. The head teacher walked into the classroom, talked with the teacher and they both turned and looked at me. At this point the room immediately grew larger and my desk appeared to be further away than before. I gulped as the head teacher walked across to my desk and asked me in his monotone voice to go to his office. I wasn't a troublesome child, but wouldn't shy away from getting into trouble, so all the way to his office I racked my brains wondering what I had done to be in this position. My mother was a governor at the school, so not only am I thinking what have I done at school, but at home also! By the time I got to the office I probably had a list of things I prepared the answer for; however, in this case the headteacher sat down at his desk, turned to his computer (black screen and green text) – I knew enough to judge we had a much better computer at home – and he asked me, 'How do I get to the next line?' He tried pressing space bar to get there, but it wasn't working. Then he went on to say how long he'd been trying to figure this out. I was probably six years old at this point, so with a smile from ear to ear I said, 'Let me see.' I looked at the keyboard, told him to press 'return' and hey presto! He turned back around in amazement. Let's say after this encounter my school 'net worth' grew among teachers with some fantastic reports on my work.

One of my traits is that I get fully immersed in anything I take a liking to, set myself a goal, or even if I 'say' I'm going to do it, I go for that task with complete focus and dedication. This tunnel focus allows me to stay on track but also allows me to dive deep into the subject matter and learn what I need to do in a short amount of time.

From a six-year-old programming in Basic to becoming a 10-year-old ready to learn C++ programming. I loved playing the PlayStation, I'm sure everybody who played one did, but I took that gaming level one step further when I managed to convince my family that I was ready for the next level of programming and I got a Net Yaroze. This was a black PlayStation that gave you the power to develop your own games. I never did create anything ground-breaking with it, similar to the Amstrad, but I learnt an awful lot, from programming in a new language to 3D modelling.

I guess the question here is why is all this relevant? Well, a six-year-old programming isn't a Guinness World Record or a never-before-seen 'thing', but it's the mindset of wanting to create something and going and creating it from a young age in an advanced manner. What this allowed me to do was engage in some topics with seniority about technology and maybe in the correct circumstances it could have led to huge great leaps, who knows. But what was important was the fact that I had a passion for tech and I was doing something with it before puberty.

Playground trading

This was really my first venture into the commercial world from a young age. Before heading to primary school, I would visit the local newsagents. I'll never forget the owner's wife, a grumpy looking lady, never smiled and eyebrows and she was always frowning. Her eyes were like slits in a watermelon. You couldn't see them, but you knew they were there. They'd follow you around the whole shop; I mean, you couldn't steal anything apart from the papers because everything was behind glass counters.

Before you could count to five she'd yell, 'What do you want?' Maybe it was just me she had this relationship with or maybe it was just the way she was.

'100 Woppa bars, please,' I'd say. '50 mint, 50 cola.' As happy as a lottery winner she'd pull the boxes out from the glass cabinet and start counting. Every Woppa bar she'd count you would think was wafer thin; there was no pulling the wool over this woman's eyes.

Now these Woppa bars were a licence to print money. They were 5p each and they would go for 20p easy in the playground. After about 10 minutes of waiting around I was armed with my stock, some of which I'd sell and some I'd give to my friends. The bottom line was, as always, news travelled that there was a salesman in the playground.

A few months later, back to the drawing board and I was contemplating what else I could sell. In the nineties, Top of the Pops was the show you watched on a Friday night, filled with all of the latest music you could guarantee from Monday all your friends would be singing the latest hits, from I Wanna Be a Hippy to Walk Like a Champion by Prince Naseem.

Well, the penny dropped, and I got the single cassette recorder/player out and recorded each song from Top of the

Pops. There I was on Friday night, having somehow managed to get myself 'alone' in front of the television and making sure there was complete silence as I held the cassette recorder close to the TV speaker. It was an art to be able to press record and play at the same time along with the pause button and not to make the 'screech' noise you'd usually hear on this sort of cassette tape. Well, the first tape sounded great, I mean there were a few muffles, but once I had my master copy created it was easy to duplicate. Straight over to the hi-fi, master cassette in the player, blank cassette in the recorder and off we go! (Sorry for those who missed out on cassettes and haven't got the foggiest what's going on here.)

The most important part of this was the presentation. No use trying to flog an 'Alba 60 mins' cassette tape with your own writing all over the stickers; it had to look professional. I decided to get my publishing skills to work and off to the PC I went. I designed a cover that read 'Lazar's Hits 96' with clip art of a DJ and a tracklist on the back. I had to show all my mates what I had in order for them to want one!

I was convinced that this looked like something you could sell at the Virgin Records shop. Let's not forget that at 10 years of age I was completely oblivious to music rights and piracy. Well, I never liked anything to do with pirates. Eye-patch? Hook? No, not for me, thank you. So I managed to convince all my friends and some punters, probably came to about 20 kids in total, to buy these cassette tapes. They bought the first one, but getting them to buy next week's top 10 didn't really work. I soon figured out this subscription business was hard work and that I was better off sticking to the sweets!

Supply & demand

It was 1999 and the terrible war in Yugoslavia was coming to an end. During this time there seemed to be a surge in Serbians coming to the UK to live. All of a sudden, I'm faced with Serbian people my own age and they know about all the things I know about (trends, TV shows, football etc) which was puzzling. I was always under the impression that they were decades behind, but later I would find out that the mindset of the older generation was that when they left, time stood still, and things never developed. So now I've actually got people I can talk to about relevant topics and get back to bringing my Serbian up to speed – result!

With the honeymoon period over, opportunities started to arise. Now, there's one story that springs to mind whenever I hear 'Blockbuster', for the very reason that with the right direction, it could become a blockbuster comedy sketch. Living in a priest's house, especially at such a time when many need direction, it is natural for the newcomers to flock to the house and ask for help, whether it is a driving licence form they need help filling out or general knowledge about the country they now live in.

One visitor in particular asked me if I could have a quiet word with him in the kitchen. 'Sure,' I replied. Now, this chap always did seem shifty in the sense that, similar to the watermelon eyes I mentioned earlier, this chap had a pair of them, and maybe I'm generalising but with a 100% hit rate it made me think there was something fishy about that appearance. Well, it turned out I had every right to think that!

So he was talking about football, the weather and all manner of things that were completely unrelated, so I butted in and said: 'What is it you want?' He sheepishly smiled, looked around the floor and didn't seem to know where to look. Now, in order to maintain this chap's anonymity, I won't say whether he was single or dating, but let's just say he wasn't alone much, which would imply that he was engaging with the opposite sex. Now, apart from the eye thing I mentioned, his English accent really wasn't doing him any favours, soft but strong Eastern European, so instead of 'Where' it sounded like 'Fair'. Not good. What made it worse was he liked to watch a certain type of film and let's say you couldn't find that sort of film on daytime television, and it turned out you couldn't watch it at night-time either. The guy had even gone to the lengths of classifying these sort of films. As a young man I was clearly confused and out of my depth here.

So, this poor chap – and I say poor because he clearly was oblivious to where he was going with this – walked into Blockbuster Video Rentals, looked around for this type of genre and realised there was none on display. Instead of asking a friend of his or even me before visiting the place (which I assume he was clearly embarrassed about), he turned to a lady who worked in store and asked her. As he was telling me this, a picture was already painted in my head and the palm of my hand was in my face with embarrassment for him. He leant over to the lady across the desk and, in the dullest, strongest but mousiest Eastern European accent he whispered, 'Do you have _____?'

To which she replied in the deepest Scottish accent: 'Are you f*#king kidding me, get the f*#k out of this shop.'

So, I laughed and after I wiped away my tears, I asked him, 'Well, what do you want me to do about it?' It turned out that he knew about these special satellite channels and we happened to have that sort of satellite. This satellite dish was about a metre in diameter, it was huge; you would think our house was picking up NASA satellites. It was used for watching European television, but we would also use it when guiding people to our house. 'As soon as you get onto our street, you'll see a big satellite dish. Yes, that's our house.'

Before you knew it, I had set up a subscription deal, £20 per 'long play' video and he wanted one per week.

So how did I do it?

Our satellite had a motor, so I'd set my alarm to wake me up at 11:30pm, go downstairs 'for a glass of water', tune into the channel, turn off the TV and hit record on the VHS player, making sure I'd be up at 5:30am to eject the videotape and move the satellite dish back to where it should be. What made it even more comical was that I wasn't even interested in the content; as long as it was all on tape, I could sell it!

It was a huge risk. If I had been caught, for sure I would have been grounded and all sorts. Could you imagine if word had got out of what the priest's son had been doing? Selling what kind of videos? Wow! So, this lasted about six months or so, sometimes with more than one a week. I mean, £300 plus for pocket change, not bad! Well, he ended up getting married and I have never seen the man since!

Growing with tech

As technology grew, I grew with it. Do you remember the first mass consumer-ready mobile phones in the UK? I recall you really had two options of network at the time, one2one and BT Cellnet (don't quote me on that, but that's my recollection). The first mobile phone I had was in 2000 and it was a Motorola MR1 mobile phone with a flip piece. I remember going to school with the phone in my inner coat pocket. Mind you, the phone itself was almost half my body size.

As more and more mobile phones came to mass market there would be opportunities ahead. I remember that within the space of a year the manufacturers managed to make phones 75% smaller, and they were becoming such a fashion accessory, especially with the introduction of mobile phone covers for Nokia mobile phones. So, in 2001 I was at the local market when I saw a new stall pop up. These guys were selling mobile phones, accessories and even unlocking mobile phones so that you could change the network you wished to use. We got talking and they told me how they had problems unlocking some phones, so I asked them what the procedure was to they unlock them. The next day I provided them with the solution to their problem; these guys were stunned! For a fairly long time over the next few years we were good friends, and I offered them support when they needed it.

eBay was the newest thing on the block in 2003 and I became an internet trading king while at university. Buying and selling stock from laptops and cameras to clothing, my university living accommodation was soon turning into a mini warehouse. A friend told me about eBay, and I wasn't too convinced that some website would bring in 'real money', but within two weeks into my first month trading and gross sales hit £7,000. I went to my bank to check it was real and the first thing the bank manager did was say, 'Can you just wait there a second?' and off she went through a door that said 'Manager's Office'. At this point I gulped and started to think, 'What's going on?' and a little sweat started to appear in my palm. After what felt like three hours but was only probably 10 minutes, she came back, with her eyes darting straight across the room as she walked across to me with a seemingly angry expression on her face.

'Is everything OK?' I asked.

'Where has this money come from?' she asked. 'eBay,' I replied.

'Why is eBay sending you money?' she said. 'Because I'm

trading on eBay,' I answered.

She handed over my statement and it was real. The money had landed. I was being asked questions at the local bank as if I had stolen the money, but at this point my initial worry turned into 'Wow, I must be on to a goldmine.'

But like most things you've got to get there early on to reap the rewards for as long as possible, and it wasn't long before the high street retailers joined eBay, and suddenly being a re-seller wasn't as lucrative as it initially had been.

What it did teach me was the speed of the internet and the power behind global transactions. People were able to buy online, any time of the day/night whenever they wanted. I know I'm sounding old, but it was all revolutionary stuff back then!

Let's just say it helped me enjoy my university life a lot more than I would have done without trading. In other words, I had a heck of a lot of fun!

My father

Those that know me will know that I talk about my late mother a lot more than I talk about my father, and I guess that's because I lost my mum, suddenly, to cancer when I was 23 and she had just turned 51. It was a part of my growing up that scarred me and shifted my whole mindset towards everything that I had ever experienced. It really was a wake-up call to how cruel life can be and also how precious life is.

My father came to the UK from Montenegro in '76 and married my mother. His wish was to become the parish priest in the town and parish, which spun over many counties. He was instrumental in the purchase of the Serbian Orthodox church in Corby when it was bought in '87, but later in 2000 he finished completing the second purpose-built Serbian Orthodox church from its foundation. Now that's such a statement of determination from the concept through to fundraising to completion. Where his determination stems from, I believe, is his faith in God. Since arriving in the UK in '76 he worked right up until '09 – that's 33 years – at the same company, British Steel. He went from washing windows to working the jackhammer to operating the road sweeper to being manager of a QA department, all while retaining the role of a parish priest. Since then he has moved to Kristiansand in Norway to oversee the construction of another Orthodox church, then he moved back to his homeland Montenegro where he is active around various monasteries serving as a priest.

I learnt a lot of lessons from my father, mainly from just shadowing him and witnessing first-hand what it is like to deal with certain situations and certain people. A lot of that was invaluable, but what really used to hit home was that he would always deliver. If he said that he would do 'X' it would always get done, and that is something I cherish. If you are to put your name to anything – whether that be paper, a business or a building – then you should always do it to your best ability and not bother doing anything half-heartedly.

My father had never built a church before. He had assisted in the acquisition of the church hall from the neighbouring Methodist hall, but he had never had any first-hand experience in construction or development. His idea behind building a separate church to what was being used came down to the fact that the hall which was acquired stayed very much the same as it was, with the installation of a wooden altar and long, tall stage curtains that would conceal the altar when not in use. As the church hall was purchased for worship, it also became a place to congregate and hold events, and my father felt uncomfortable with the idea of the altar being covered with curtains and people smoking, drinking and acting in a way, let's say, that you wouldn't act in church. So, 10 years after the purchase in around '98, he started the project of building the church.

Once he made the decision you could say he ran with it. Gathering information, architectural drawings, fundraising, tradesmen, specialists, you name it. Of course, he was greatly supported by many, but he was the driving force behind this brainchild. I believe what everybody saw in him was the passion he had for making this church a spiritual place of worship which wouldn't be interfered with by functions/parties. But it was the passion and belief that he had within himself. I often see this in people whether performing on stage or acting on set, when you are able to identify a special gift that somebody has. How they are able to be consistent at this one thing is truly amazing. This has never really applied to me as I'm constantly in different areas of business, but I've realised that my passion lies within business itself, regardless of sector.

My father came to the UK not knowing English, he worked in a full-time job, provided for the family and also was the longest ever serving parish priest, who was instrumental in acquiring one church and building another before going on to other parishes in other counties. Now, although my father isn't commercially focused, he has strong beliefs in what he does, he's a do-er and someone who 'makes it happen' – to me, not only because he is my father but because he's someone who puts ideas into action, I tip my hat to you, father, and I am immensely proud of what you have achieved in life.

CHAPTER

3

Off into the real world

It was 2006 and I'd just graduated from university with a degree in accounting and finance. I was relieved that I'd completed that hurdle, but still I was not feeling fulfilled, partly because I realised that I went to university to tick a box in the family, but I didn't really like studying the subject. I remember enrolling at university looking at the list of subjects I could choose, and nothing was really attractive about any of the subjects. I had a love for business, and I guess I thought, 'Well, accounting and finance is all about numbers, planning and forecasting, so I'll give it a go.' Don't get me wrong, the education was priceless, and although at the time I may not have realised where and how I'd apply it in practice, the lessons learned surely did pay dividends later on in life when I got out there and started my own businesses.

During my final term I received a visit from my cousin in

Belgrade. He flew into the UK for a short break and we did the whole touristy thing around London and cried with laughter as we watched the film Borat. One topic he brought up was around real estate in Serbia and Montenegro. He was a self-made entrepreneur in electronics with a discipline, and his style and mannerisms always screamed 'business mode on'. Whether he was on a business call or shopping for shoes, you could be sure he would treat each task with the same discipline. Not buying it? Then let me tell you about shoe shopping with him in London.

What shop does every tourist want to visit when in London? That's right, the famous green bag with the gold letters, the famous department store Harrods. There he was, in the middle of Harrods like a kid in a candy shop. My cousin was out to buy some stylish clothes, you know, the sort of thing that would be a conversation topic: 'Yeah, you like these? I bought them while I was in London.' This was the sort of topical conversation I was about to explore; I just was completely unaware at the time.

We headed over to the shoes, and if you were to ask me, I'd have said the whole top row looked completely the same. He picked up one shoe in a certain style I find hard to explain, as if it were a porcelain vase. He had one hand on the heel of the shoe and the other hand holding the tip, he would rotate the shoe in a 180-degree fashion and look at this shoe as if he was waiting for a reaction from the shoe itself. I found it ever so puzzling! After about one minute, although it felt like five, of him assessing the shoe, I suggested, 'Perhaps you could try it on?'

'No,' he said. 'No.' It was one of those moments when you're having fun and for one reason or another the mood completely shifts to serious and you start to feel a little on edge, like something's not quite right.

I stepped back and watched from a distance, as he went to another shoe and performed the same 'ritual'. At this point I learnt that entrepreneurs are not your 'norm' and they have a certain form or quirkiness to them. My cousin was all about detail and while he was looking at this shoe for perhaps an error or a sign of approval, I realised then that this is how he operates: whether it's work or play, he has the same personality and the same thought process. Usually you'd associate a wealthy person with going shopping, picking stuff up and buying it without looking twice; I guess that's from watching too many films, or perhaps those that do that didn't earn the money via a similar level of hardship.

As for my cousin, living in Belgrade he was at the heart of the bombing which took place in the nineties. It was still fresh, he had seen a lot and managed to get through the other end still being in business. I admired him a lot, he was hard as rock, a tough guy, but with a heart of gold.

'Let's go,' he said, and we walked out of Harrods without any green bag whatsoever; I was stunned. We visited various stores on Bond Street where he bought some garments, we had a walk around Hyde Park, visited the London Eye, did the whole touristy thing. Before we headed back home, he said, 'Let's go back to Harrods.' What transpired was that the whole day he thought about those shoes and decided he wanted to go back to the store to buy them. What I loved about this was that he wouldn't rush any decision just to have that satisfaction of a 'win'. At 20 years old, I was the complete opposite; 'impulsive' was my middle name, but I learnt a valuable lesson from him on decision-making: no matter how big or small the decision may be, treat it with the same seriousness.

During his stay we spoke a lot about real estate and the potential in Montenegro. It had just become an independent state, which meant in real estate terms the potential was 'fresh' for foreign investment. I loved talking business with my cousin, or should I say listening to him share his thoughts and experiences. I found that listening was so much more powerful than waffling on or saying something perhaps just for the sake of it, as you'd lose the core message.

As time went by, our conversation would play on my mind, so I started to reach out to real estate agencies to see what they were offering in the area. I felt that there was an opportunity for me to create something here. Meanwhile my father was, as any father would be, concerned about my career post university. Just before I was due to graduate he would probe to find out what my train of thought was post studies. In line with my mother, his view was that I should get a job with a steady income. To me it really wasn't what I wanted to do as I had this burning desire to 'take on the world', and getting on the career ladder seemed like a safe bet. I justified this by saying that as I had not taken a gap year during university, I figured I had one year to explore. I did apply for a graduate scheme at the company my father worked at, which by then had changed hands several times, to Corus first and then TATA Steel. I applied for the job, got through to the second-round interview and for one reason or another they withdrew the job listing. To me this was the best sign I could have wished for.

So off I went on my journey into real estate with no experience whatsoever.

I started off by registering a company and creating an investment prospectus online. This investment prospectus was showing off some real serious investments from half a million euros upwards, from private acquisitions to privatisations. I was a reader of the Financial Times during my studies, and I figured this was exactly where I needed to be! After some negotiating with an advertising executive of the FT, there it was, V-Property, featured in the House and Home weekend edition of the FT. Calls and emails started to come in; these were from anyone from private investors to hedge fund managers, so all of a sudden I felt that I was in the deep end, but I was there and I was swimming!

As the relationships in investment started to develop, so did my ideas. I was now entering serious negotiations with the investors, and there was a clear appetite for some of the big boys to enter the market. The next stage of developing the business was to build my own real estate to sell. My father had a lot of family land around the coast and in the mountains in Montenegro, so we agreed on a fairly small plot to get started with. The idea was to construct holiday homes for tourists and sell them off-plan, a simple and smooth way to get things going. When I was discussing this model with various people in Montenegro, they were looking at me as if I had fallen from the sky. 'You want to build it, then sell it,' they'd say. 'How can you sell something that's not even built yet?' This was such a culture wake-up call on Eastern meets Western practice. I was surrounded by so much potential that I started to grow and grow, all by spotting opportunities in the market and adapting them to fit a model that would work.

It wasn't all rosy, however. During the personal project of building apartments, I opened an office in the UK with a sales team, one in Belgrade, one in Moscow and one in Montenegro. Deals were coming in; however, I felt the biggest 'hit' on one of the biggest deals I was about to secure. Picture a 21-year-old closing a €12m deal for a ski resort; it was epic. Long story short, a UK property magnate in the care home industry sold up and was spreading his investments around the world from Panama to Montenegro. After picking up what we were doing in the Financial Times, he called us up and headed over for a meeting. All necessary checks were in place and the investor didn't seem at the outset to be a time waster. A team of us booked tickets, and the next day we were out in Montenegro evaluating potential investments and returns.

The investor was a fairly wacky guy, a very short and

plump Indian man, and some of his stories and comments he would come out with would make you think, 'What?' He had this trait of smiling, showing his teeth and saying 'lemon fresh' with a strong Indian accent. He seemed to be a bit of a showman, but I figured that at 74 years of age, he was just letting his hair down and enjoying life after a lot of hard work. This is where the young me failed to pick up on different characters in business and how they react to situations, as what became clear was that the investor used the opportunity of visiting the investments to try to create connections of his own with his 'friendly' manner to effectively try to shove me out of the picture. After the trip we discussed options and negotiated for months, and he eventually pulled out of the investments, saying he wasn't going to invest in real estate. Personally, at the time I didn't take it as a bad thing. I figured you can't win them all, no big deal.

Six months later, I'm in Moscow at one of the world's prominent international real estate exhibition displaying my projects to potential investors, and I see this short, plump Indian dude walking around and I can't believe it. Before I could say anything, he said, 'Didn't expect to see me here?' We exchanged pleasantries and arranged a meeting, and during that meeting I'm thinking to myself, 'What have I done to deserve this?' Basically, it seemed to me that he was trying to buy back my interest/relationship by mapping out different investments he would be willing to make with me. Although I was young, I wasn't shy, so not so politely I told him what I could offer, and I said that some of these fairy-tale investments he was trying to create as a distraction simply would never happen.

After the show my Montenegrin team found out that the said investor had in fact started to invest in building a seaside resort. He didn't invest in the larger portfolio I had offered, but he seemed to be active. The client refused to pay the commission on the deal to me until the investor had completed the whole sales process, which was fair. We chased up on the commission and never got it, and within a few months the Middle Eastern client who I was representing on the deal vanished from Montenegro, and the seaside resort still sits there until this day as land.

The lesson learnt here was if you feel warning signs and things don't add up, then don't waste your time trying to be Sherlock Holmes and find out why. Take yourself away and invest your time where you will receive benefit.

As far as bad news goes, I started to receive reports that some people in the sales team were registering deals in their personal name behind my back and pocketing the commission. It amounted to almost €80,000, and that was just from one employee. With a team of eight I couldn't say hand on heart that they were all clean after this, nor could I ever suggest that others were. It was a very disappointing lesson to learn that people you were paying a good wage and treating like family were stealing from you.

I was 22 years old when the global economic downturn hit.

Everybody was talking recession, the famous Russian investors were now nowhere to be seen and a few Middle Eastern hedge funds that were clients of mine around Montenegro disappeared, and to make it worse my mother got diagnosed with terminal lung cancer. I decide to throw in the towel, wind everything up and spend as much time as I could with my mother for the remainder of her life.

Keep the drinks flowing

Having spent the best part of eight months committed to my mother, we ended up losing her in July 2009, just after her 51st birthday. The heartache I experienced at that time was something that I cannot even try to explain. At 23 years old, I had always wanted to provide my mother with a palatial home and life of luxury, as she was the most selfless lady I think the world has ever seen. From sending humanitarian aid to her home country, to raising her children, to working all the hours that God sent, she always had time for everyone but herself, and it was my lifelong ambition that one day I would give her a life fit for a queen. As a young and ambitious man at the time, I was a little blinded by all that glitters, but my feet were always firmly on the ground, and on reflection it would have been great if I'd had a mentor for my real estate business, as they would have been able to guide me through the process and I wouldn't necessarily have had to find out what the process was, learn about it, then go through it. What I'm saying is, time is so important, it's the only commodity in this world that is priceless. Most things that you spend, you can buy back, but not time. And that's why I tend to keep a strict plan of my time where possible to ensure I'm not throwing good time after bad at any point in my life.

It took me a while to come to terms with what I had just been through after the burial, but I needed to get back to work. I felt disconnected from the world, numb. I knew that getting back to work would help the healing process, and I could shift my focus from reminiscing on my life with my mother, dwelling on what I could have done, what I should have done; I really was in a bad place. The only activity I was really doing was going to the gym to train. I found this to be another place of worship for me as I'd get there and switch off from everything that was going on in life, and pumping iron/exercising was that focused concentration on something that would bring me relief. I met a bunch of friends for life at the gym I was using, and I'd drive a good 30 minutes just to get to that place. It was my secret getaway from anything close to me.

After workouts there would be a bar area where we'd all drink our protein/recovery shakes and catch up. I remember the topic being about beer one day. One of the guys was explaining how he loved beer and would visit festivals in the UK, but then he would go on about Bavaria and the Bavarian history of beer and about all the different tastes and how the water would make such a difference to the taste of the beer itself. I wasn't really a fan of beer/lager or any alcohol really, but for some reason what my friend had to say on the subject really captured my interest.

So, I went home, I researched and I realised it was a lucrative business. But what could I do in this domain?

After brainstorming for hours on end, it came to my attention that there was a beer in Montenegro that had won various awards at European beer festivals but had never been sold in the UK market. Well, that was enough to get me interested. I visited the factory, had a tour of how their production is set out and their capabilities, I became immersed in their company, their history and their ethos – you could say they had my buy-in!

I remember all of the staff within this small town in Montenegro being very proud of what the company had achieved in almost 100 years. For me it was great to see happy people behind a company you've just met; that left such a lasting impression on me. One of

the secrets to the beer's success was the water, which was this mountain spring water that alone just really tasted fantastic. I left the company with a gentleman's agreement that I would be taking a trial order very soon, and off I went.

Of course, I wouldn't have come all this way just to visit a brewery. While researching beer I was also researching wines and spirits; I was deep into the market to see what was on offer, and I was tallying up costs of import, duty and excise on customs costs. There was this one wine that I always remember my father mentioning at various dinner parties. If it hasn't become apparent already, well, people from Montenegro tend to be proud people. We would only offer you the best grape, the best barley, you name it. Whatever it may be, it had to be the best!

This one wine was found in the nineties in a supermarket in the UK called Safeway. Whenever we'd do our family grocery shopping, my father would go to the wine isle to buy a few bottles of red wine from Montenegro, called Vranac. Now, I'm not 100% sure, but I'm pretty certain he would use this red wine as part of the holy communion in church. Why? Because it was the best!

The main reason why this wine wasn't available in the UK anymore was due to the sanctions imposed during the nineties and the troubles in Yugoslavia. While on this fact-finding mission, I felt I had to visit the company in question as it may be an opportunity too good to miss. There I was in Montenegro, ready to go into a meeting with the director of their export operations. Similar to the brewery visit, it was pretty standard stuff: company history, product range and current operations. We parted ways and I promised to be in touch soon.

Back in England, I was busy number crunching and calling around wholesalers, supermarkets, some specialist wine/beer stores and even some pubs trying to sell them 'the best'. It really wasn't easy cold calling all of these places, but doing all of this was helping me out incredibly. My confidence was coming back, I was starting to enjoy life again regardless of the amount of 'No, sorry, not interested' responses I was getting from my calls. I felt like I was doing something good, something positive and that this business had legs!

Through a friend of a friend of a friend, I found myself in this enormous bonded warehouse in the UK full of alcohol. These two brothers might as well have been named 'Alco' and 'Hol' – they were the big boys in the game; there was nothing that these guys didn't know about booze. What's more is that they used to visit my part of the world in the seventies and eighties on their trade visits. What really made me connect with these guys was that they were so down to earth and really helpful. We sat down for hours and discussed importing bottled water, wine, spirits, beer, the lot. It really was one of those meetings where you know you're going to end up doing some business somewhere down the line.

Three weeks later and you can hear the truck backing up ready to unload 33 pallets of beer to the guys I've just mentioned. They took a variety of beer to trial. Alongside that, a supermarket chain in the UK was trialling the wine as their own label brand to their subscribers on the wine list. Things were good, I was trading and managing to get business growing. Then, a brick wall for the beer: it tasted good, but the alcohol volume needed to come down to make it work for the volume. The drinks trade is based on tight margins and high volume; this was in the early days of the craft breweries which were taking off in the UK, but they weren't where they are today. The beer had to come down 2.5% in alcohol volume to make commercial sense on import and distribution costs. To me it seemed a no-brainer, but to the Montenegrins it was a no-go. They couldn't do it without impacting the taste of the beer, it just wouldn't get that complexity. So, they started to work on an export beer, which I think they're still working on today!

I must admit this was not one of my most exciting ventures in the business world, but I learnt that I really had a passion for trading, so much so that I'd personally get in a van and drive orders around the country to customers from Grimsby to London. There was something about trading, negotiating and getting a deal that I loved. I managed to retain the distribution rights after trading the brands for a number of years, but with no large volume orders it wasn't a scalable business in the UK. I realised that I had a passion for trade, but not so much for the alcohol side. I wasn't a wine connoisseur at the end of the day, so I decided to get out of this business and look further afield.

4

Once a toy boy...

T oys, toys, toys! We all love them, and as we grow old, we still have our fond memories of our favourite toys. The toys we would never let go of, the toys that went everywhere with us, from school to bedtime. I remember as a child the Saturday treat would be for Mum or Dad to buy me a toy, and where was the home for toys in the nineties? That's right, Woolworths! I remember walking into that shop as a kid and entering some sort of zombie mode as I'd magically appear in front of all these toys that I just needed in my life! If you had told me then that in around 15 to 20 years' time I would have my own toy shop next door, I'd have probably pooped with excitement!

I was worried of falling into some sort of limbo with business after the drinks trade, and I wanted a new challenge, but I felt that I was hitting some sort of wall. Literally there didn't seem to be much going on; I remember walking through the town shopping centre one day and spotting this vacant, very small kiosk-type retail unit. I stopped and thought to myself, 'What could I do in there?' It wasn't something I had ever thought of doing, being a shopkeeper, but I guess subconsciously I enjoyed trading so much. And as it had all been B2B up to that point, I thought that I'd try trading with the general public in retail. So, I enquired about the premises costs, and when asked, 'What would you like to do with the unit space?' my reply was, 'I don't know!'

I was on a shopping trip with my then girlfriend and noticed this 'gyro helicopter' whizzing around. Like most big kids, I stopped and marvelled at this helicopter which was floating incredibly well inside a shopping centre, and the movement/control of this thing was fantastic. I had to have one. As I walked into the shop, I noticed so many different gadgets, gifts and novelties that I had never seen before. I think it was the first time ever I had been in a gadget store. I fell in love, I loved it and I wanted one – not the helicopter this time, I wanted my own gadget shop!

A few days later, there I was back in my hometown, staring at this empty space which was going to be my gadget shop, my first venture into retail. I was trying to plan how I was going to fit all of that stock into a shop that was probably around 4 metres by 2 metres – I was puzzled, but there was a small fire burning inside me for this project. It was late October 2010 with Christmas around the corner, so I knew I had to move fast. Day after day I was reaching out to wholesalers and product owners, trying to get the coolest gifts and products I could source just in time for when I planned to open. There was instant snow in a can, a dumbbell alarm clock (10 reps to turn it off), a self-stirring mug, money toilet roll and the all-important helicopter range – I managed to fill the shop with everything you'd want for a gadget shop of that size, and it was to be the only one in town … well, that's what I thought.

The shop was open, and I'd regularly stand outside and welcome punters in, almost like a market stall. I just loved that feeling of trading (I've got to stop saying this!). I named the shop 'The Biz', because of my dealing with the Montenegrins – the sense of being proud rubbed off on me and the shop would have to be 'The Biz' for anyone to go in. However, the news travelled fast, and people were flocking into the shop to have a 'nosey' and see what it was all about. It was really well received, and business was booming for such a small operation. One day, however, I heard a kid in the shop say to his friends, 'Let's go have a look at the other gadget shop.'

'Hold on a minute, what other gadget shop?' I said. 'Hawkin's Bazaar,' they said and off they went.

'Hawkin's Bazaar,' I said to myself, 'What's that?' At the end of the day, I locked up and thought I'd have a walk through town, and after wandering around for a while I found it. There it was in all its glory: big, bright and modern. Probably about 15 of my shops could have fitted inside it. 'Opening Tomorrow,' it said in the window. I could see a team of people inside working to stock the shelves. My emotions were completely mixed, from angry to intrigued to almost thinking, 'That's what I want!'

Well, the next day, the town was full of these bright yellow bags with Hawkin's Bazaar written all over them, while I was in a pigeonhole in the other end of town with not as much going on as on the previous days, and that was all thanks to the big shot in town! During December I'd do what most would do (I imagine): I'd take a walk across to see how well they were trading. The more I looked at the store in awe, the more I was processing information I didn't even know I was doing. I was analysing everything about the store from the POS, display, layout of products, flow of customers. But you just couldn't transfer any of this stuff to such a small operation as mine as it wasn't scalable. I found out that the store was a temporary store too just over Christmas (to clean up on the Christmas retail spend), which was a pain as it was the classic scenario of two buses turning up at the same time after a long period of none. Nevertheless, I decided it was time to get talking with the manager of the store. He turned out to be an incredibly nice man and shared some really good insight as to how they were doing. I'll never forget how I left the store with my tail between my legs thinking, 'How could they take so much money in one day?' I really couldn't believe the business they were doing. For those that don't know, Hawkin's Bazaar is a novelty store and they've been around for a long time. They sell a lot of stocking fillers, simple toys;

they are a one-stop shop for Christmas, basically.

It was almost Christmas and we had so much snow that you just couldn't believe it. As I'm watching the snow settle, it was almost like those cartoons you see of hallucinations; it was like I was seeing money fall from the sky. 'Sledges!' I thought to myself and in an instant I was on the phone trying to get a hold of as many sledges as possible. I think I bought 200 or 300 sledges altogether, and I managed to convince a chap across the road to store them for me on the proviso that he got one sledge for free in return. Well, these sledges were moving fast, and in the end I was the only retailer in the town with sledges as the snow was so bad it caused a logistical nightmare around the country. It only meant one thing for me, that the price went up due to demand, each day! I remember the parents coming in and looking at the prices of these sledges in horror and attempting to leave the shop. But their child would then cry because they wanted a sledge and there was nowhere else they could get them. OK, this was a bit extreme, and you could say I was comparable to Ebenezer Scrooge, but that's when I had the big lightbulb moment.

Toy boy

'I'm going to open a toy shop.'

There was no single place in the town dedicated to toys. Woolworths was gone and the other stores that would sell toys wouldn't have a large range of products. This was it, a toy shop! I always wanted a toy shop! Off I went, looking around the town for a suitable premises to house my next venture, and there I was, stood outside the very same shop (Woolworths) I used to visit every Saturday as a child. The store next to it was available. Of course, it wasn't as big as Woolworths; I think it was almost 2,000 sq. ft, which for what I had in mind was great. Christmas was over, The Biz had been a success, but for such a small town it wasn't an all-year-round shop, so it had to go. It had served its purpose and now I was moving on to bigger and better things. Building from that experience, I got stuck into my next venture. It was January and I had already booked my visit to London's Toy Fair to see what all the fuss was about.

I was 25 years old and excited that I was going to a toy fair, so you can see what I meant about my inner child still being well and truly alive. When I arrived I saw mascots walking around everywhere, everyone from Teenage Mutant Ninja Turtles to Bugs Bunny. I was so happy I couldn't believe it, and from that point on I knew I wanted to be involved in the toy industry in one way or another. I spent the whole day at the toy fair literally going from one stand to another, doing my research, learning about what each company had to offer and how I could work with them, and I shared my ambitions about opening a toy store. This sector was such a breath of fresh air, a complete shift from the real estate sector. I wasn't talking to people about returns on investments or stressing to a constructor that a deadline had to be met or penalties will follow. I was talking to people who were genuinely in love with their products. There was that sense of happiness in everybody there; they all seemed to be having fun and I loved it!

I had viewed the store I planned on taking on, I had all the measurements and floor plans, and I was designing my own store layout. I was thinking about where the shelving would go, how high the racking would be, what products would sit where and how the store would be laid out in sections (pre-school, Lego, etc). I was 100% immersed in what I was doing. One of the hardest parts after the toy fair was the product selection. I was completely out of my depth trying to decide what to pick. I was in no man's land, I had no clue where to go or who to turn to. When I managed to get in touch with some experts, they did say that it's down to your judgement, which didn't really help. So, off I went with my own judgement of what might sell and what might not, and boy was it difficult! The selection was covering everything from puzzles, board games, pre-school, construction, dolls, role-play, you name it. One interesting concept I decided to bring on board was similar to that famous store where you can build your own teddy bear. I basically designed a very similar concept, albeit a little bit easier on the pocket, which was beautifully designed. It was called 'Make Your Own Bear' and it had everything from the bear selection, sound selection, stuffing machine, clothing, dresser and adoption centre where you print off your own certificate and receive your teddy bear in a box. What I wanted to do with this store was to bring entertainment into retail. Rather than retail just being shelf, product, till, I wanted to bring a watered-down version of Hamleys to a small rural town and create a great experience for parents and children alike.

It was at this time that the name 'Toy Town' was born, along with the tag line: 'Where fun doesn't grow old!' My vision was to have a Toy Town in most towns across the UK, similar to a sort of 'Card Factory' concept, a scalable business which can adapt to the population/size of store.

I didn't really have a clue what I was doing, but I knew what I wanted, so I 'Made It Happen!'

There I am back in the landlord's office of the shopping centre, trying to negotiate a deal. The amount of money they wanted was crazy: over six figures for a year's rent and rates. I think at this point, most would pull back and retreat to the drawing board, because with all the fixtures and fittings, stock, etc it was going to cost a quarter of a million just to start. I started to think, this is a big gamble: what happens if I open the doors and nobody buys my goods? What do I do then? How do you pay the rent? Staff? Anyone that has ever worked with me when forecasting knows that it's one task I really don't like doing: putting my finger in the air and trying my best to guess the temperature. Well, before I even started to forecast, I had a pretty good idea of what amount of money needed to be taken each week in order to just break even, and as scary as it all was, I still wanted to go for it!

I had instructed a lawyer and we were back and forth with the lease for some time. I was trying to negotiate a good deal, but the appetite wasn't there from their side; they didn't want to play ball. I learnt a lot about leases when I opened my first office with V-Property, and from then on I was fine. However, for whatever reason, this deal was so rigid that in the end I walked away. It hurt to do so, but I also knew that it just wouldn't make sense to do a deal that would be a recipe for disaster. So I got to work and visited other towns, other shopping centres, and I was very much still on the hunt to get what I wanted. However, nothing seemed perfect like that one retail unit. It was so perfect it even had snakes and ladders floor graphics (it was a former Adams Kids clothes store). Weeks passed by, then months, and I was no closer to securing a retail premises for my 'baby'.

One day I was driving to the gym when I saw a call come in from the property agent for the retail unit I wanted. I took the call and found out that the whole shopping centre complex was being sold and there was a deal to be done – a deal so good that I should come to the office ASAP. I told him I'll bring my lawyer to the meeting and we can complete the deal at the table. My excitement at this point was through the roof. I had a feeling that it was all about to happen! I arrived at the office and entered a boardroom with approx. eight people, and there was me, this scruffy 25-year-old trader. The first question I posed to them was: 'How do I know you guys are serious?' At this point their portfolio director slammed his pen down, loosened his tie and said, 'We're not here to dick around.' Instantly I felt like the golden goose at the table. After letting my inner child laugh away for a moment as I struggled to contain my excitement, I then breathed in and got down to business. What felt like a few hours later, I left the meeting having secured a deal that I don't think many independent traders have ever managed to get. The lawyers started talking and I had the keys in a matter of weeks.

Toy Town was soon under construction, with local carpenters employed to create bespoke furniture as well as national fit-out companies. employees were hired and trained, the stock arrived and we were good to go! There was a queue outside on opening day, the doors opened, and a flood of people rushed in. I couldn't explain the joy on my face, seeing these people happy that there was a 'proper toy shop' in town. The tills were ringing and at close I couldn't believe the amount of money I was counting! It was a success!

One thing I really loved about retail was that you could adapt and react to almost anything. Whether it be seasonal or a craze, you could really move at speed, and I think that's what made the place so successful. It was that in-store entertainment, the TVs showing product adverts, the live demonstrations, competitions, all of that fun! As we approached our first Christmas, I decided to create a Santa's grotto. For £5, you'd get to see Santa, a small gift and a photo. As you can imagine, this was another jackpot with queues forming way out of the store. We closed our first Christmas quarter so strongly that I'd literally never seen so much cash in my life!

Naturally, the post-Christmas period was quiet, and January was a slow month post sales, so this was when I implemented online sales, as until now (2011) we had just been selling in store. I had some online experience from my university days of trading online, but not with 2,000 items and this kind of stock level. It seemed like a mammoth task, but one I took on with gusto. We started selling online on three platforms: Amazon, eBay and Play. Amazon was by far the strongest; as soon as we turned online sales on, it was like a tap running in a sink with a plug in. The orders were constantly coming in, but we outgrew the local post office in one week and rushed to get a dedicated daily courier collection, more hires and a different working schedule. The retail unit had one whole floor of space where we started to operate from, and I'd come in at 4 or 5 am to start picking and packing. That was when I realised I needed to now be less hands on and grow, and so we did – to three sites and a warehouse.

Looking at the market, I could see it was becoming a race to get the famous 'buy box' on Amazon. Resellers were clearly making a loss, stores were ticking over, but I was now hungrier than ever to go big or go home. I managed to get in touch with a duo who had recently done an acquisition and sale of the UK's largest pet store at the time, for £1 billion. The partner had a financial background and knew his toys, so a meeting was set up at the famous members' club 'George' in Mayfair with a view to discuss investment opportunities. I just love London, it's a magical city, the best in the world, and making a trip into the city on this day was so significant for me. I was on my way to discuss a big deal about an 'idea' I had – and thinking about it now, I still can't believe it happened! The meeting was as sharp as you'd expect: we discussed the operations, P&L, etc, it was like a Dragon's Den show, but I loved talking business! The takeaway was that they were interested, and we would keep in touch over the coming weeks to see if there was an opportunity for them. I came out of that meeting with my nose so high that it almost hit an aeroplane in the sky – what a day!

Over the coming weeks I couldn't sleep. We were exchanging information and talking, and we were going into details about how 300 stores would operate. After approximately one month, I received the dreaded email that basically said, 'We don't see a future in the UK high street for retail, it'll be more for leisure. Only retail parks and online will work, so we're out and good luck.' This news almost broke me; I felt completely shattered for months afterwards. I lost passion, lost interest in the business and with that it started to crumble. It was now heading for a downward spiral.

I never really recovered from that point with this business, as the whole journey had been difficult, but this for me was going to be the 'big win', the one that would elevate it to the level where I'd want it to be. I was very tough on myself over this period, which of course wasn't good when you're already a pretty self-critical character. I could see a change in me as a person, which started to have a knock-on effect on everything else in my life. This 'lost deal' was a domino to the business due to the way I handled it, as with lost interest in a business and not even hiring someone to run it, I had imprinted it as a failure and wanted to move on.

I closed down the high street stores as I figured there was no future in them as the experts said, and I moved to a warehouse to focus solely on online sales. Turnover was huge, profits not so big, but it allowed me to diversify into selling pretty much anything within reason online. However, within a few months, still feeling disappointed, I realised I had lost all interest in the trade.

I've got to say that this business is one that I still have the best memories from. I was able to bring something to my hometown, employ local and engage locally. Then, visiting the other stores and communities just made me feel closer to people in general and for that reason I always support local independent traders.

5

Did somebody say party?

S o, having lost interest in building a mini toy empire, I was planning to take over the world with something else, and what's the best way to move forward? Throw parties! I started organising concerts and club nights, flying in popstars from Serbia - you could say I organised a few iconic nights in the Serbian community that would last forever.

This actually started while I was still in toys, and it was helping me ease the monotony of the business. There was a growing community of Serbs in the UK, and for a while there really hadn't been any activity and events for people of our age. Growing up, these so-called 'get-togethers' would mainly be in a local community hall of sort. You know the type: plain walls, wooden floors, square – these were not flamboyant by any means, but the best thing about the décor was that nobody cared! The main reason was for people in the community to get together and talk, dance, drink and have a good time.

As a child these nights were iconic. You would meet relatives you never knew you had, but they were your mother's uncle's wife's sister's kids? – somehow you were related and as time went on, everybody was a cousin of yours, which also meant your choices would get limited when it came to trying to impress the opposite sex. During these evenings, you would just run around playing hide and seek or 'tig' while the older lot were in a circle dancing to folk music being played by a chap pulling apart an accordion, and a keyboard player mimicking the theme tune to Playbus. Circle dancing? Yeah, I'm sure you've seen the film Borat and I'd say he nails it in his version of 'Disco Dancing'. Anyway, occasionally you'd join in, but you'd get bored quickly. The middle was usually a place to hide or a safe place to hold hands and join in if you were about to get your ass kicked!

However, by the time I was in my mid-twenties, the folk nights were still happening but in smaller numbers, and the sense of community among people my age was fading slowly. With the birth of YouTube, you were able to listen to music and watch up-to-date videos and guess what? Yep, Serbians all over the world were now up to date with music and trends, and they weren't circle dancing as much as you might think.

So, my latest idea was born: I'd bring over a singer to attract the younger generation and throw a party. So it happened: the first gig was about to take place, I had arranged for friends to collect the singer and I'd put together a small team to operate the event, which wasn't so difficult as most of them were attracted to her! The evening was a success, Serbians/Non-Serbians came from all over to a nightclub in Leicester, and we had a fantastic evening!

This quickly snowballed and we held some evenings without popstars but with a really good DJ instead! Our following grew and so did the names of the artists I was bringing over. One of the most iconic evenings was when we dressed up one of those glamourous halls I mentioned and transformed it into a nightclub. People were literally walking into the place with their mouths wide open, shocked – it was a wow factor and a great first impression to the evening. The singer we had was hugely popular, and to this day I'm not quite clear on how many people were actually in the hall, but it was a lot and of course from a health and safety view we were fine! The singer and six bandmates sounded out of this world, the crowd loved it and it was at this point that a real sense of accomplishment started to set in.

As much as I was enjoying partying away, I had to shell out quite a bit of money for these singers as they needed visas, flights, etc. So I thought to myself, 'How can I monetise this better?' Those who have run events before know the risks of making that one night a success; it doesn't come easy. After a lot of thought, the lightbulb moment happened! 'I'll make them a music video while they're here.' I mean, who would turn down a music video in London? Not many artists, and that became a bargaining tool of mine when negotiating new acts!

I'll never forget the first-ever music video that I produced for an artist who I brought over for a concert. It was a moment when I threw myself into the deep end completely not knowing how to swim (not that this was unusual to me). I mean I had an A* in Media Studies at A-Level – of course I could produce a music video for a popstar! Well, let's say the penny dropped when a bald middle-aged singer started to have a hissy fit because he realised I was 'winging it'.

'That is not a video camera,' he said. 'That's a camera for photography.'

I translated his remark to the cameraman.

'Tell him, there is nothing wrong with this camera and it shoots perfectly well. I take fantastic photos of my dog with this, and I've also recorded a short movie for a friend who's studying film at university,' the cameraman said.

You can tell from this that I also didn't put any pressure on the cameraman by telling him how much of a big shot this singer was to Serbians and how he didn't realise how big this project could be. Let's just say the advantage I had was that I was the translator and, of course, I translate fully on my interpretation, right?

'He says that this is the newest camera out, you're the first popstar in the UK to be recorded with such technology. The west is so far advanced, and you'll probably see this sort of equipment back home in the next five to ten years. Wait until you see the end result, you'll thank me later.'

That toned down the hissy fit for the rest of the shoot and

we were in complete control. The cameraman was oblivious to the popstar and thinking it's his mate 'Dave' who wants to make it big. Well there was that obliviousness, but I also liked the attitude of the cameraman, he didn't give a shit. The skeleton crew I had assembled were really there for show, to make it a look a little grander than it actually was. I mean, of course you needed someone for hair and makeup, but we only had makeup – the artist didn't have any hair!

We shot this music video in various locations from a stately home to Scotland Yard, and the end result, believe it or not, was mind-blowing! Not only because we managed to wing it from start to finish, but because during the shoot my brother-in-law who was playing a criminal in the music video couldn't get his hands out of the prop handcuffs we had hired, and there was no key in sight. Along with another actor dressed as a policeman, looking all official in uniform they ended up in front of a house of a collector of memorabilia in the hope he had a key to release my brother-in-law. Could you imagine the look on the chap's face opening the door? What about his neighbourhood credibility after that! Well, let's just say not many people knew about this disaster that was going on while we were back at set shooting the music video.

The fact that we had approximately 50 people involved in such a short space of time around the Serbian community was almost like a party-type event I had been throwing. The feeling among the community and all those involved was at an all-time high. Could you imagine being a fan of an artist's music, then that artist does a gig in your local town, then you end up taking part in his music video?

That was another milestone for me. Nobody had ever done anything like this before, shot a music video with a Serbian star and have people in the community involved. There were so many 'first time' check boxes along the journey which made it even more 'ground-breaking'.

The result was that I had created a music video which racked up 1m views in a matter of days (which at the time was pretty impressive) and still to this day remains his top video on YouTube with over 11m views! The video gained national coverage in Serbia, and the PR it got was great. It was a big cigar moment for me!

What was the next stage? Incorporation! I registered LV Productions, purchased a load of equipment and we were off, filming from helicopters to private jets, to yachts – one thing that I really loved about doing this was the freedom of creativity (within the client's budget of course). But being able to picture something in your head and then 'televise' it was an art. When you got it right you felt great, but when it wasn't quite right … it still felt pretty good.

Picture this: you get sent a song, you listen to it a lot, like 100 times easily, and you start creating a story. That was how I'd start my creative process, I felt like a child with so much creativity, it was a wonderful feeling and in some cases a luxury to sit and do this while making a living from it.

So the song I was scripting a music video for was one

of those Dan Bilzerian 'look at me and my lifestyle' type of songs. This meant the budget had to be there, including the private jet and yacht! By the time I put together the treatment I called the artist, and he was more excited than a kid in a candy shop.

Two days later we were meeting a guy who could secure us a private jet for filming. Imagine you are in Eastern Europe and in a café that has seen better days (to put it politely), and you've got someone promising you that they can secure a private jet. I know if it was any of my friends at the time, they would have told me to move on and that this guy probably couldn't deliver a paper plane if his life depended on it. Well, this guy, dressed in tracksuit bottoms, gold bracelets, chains and the all-important leather jacket, was adamant that he could deliver, and he was also a big fan of the artist.

'It's ready' he said. 'Let's go.'

Off he went, leading the way as I followed him in my car. To picture it a little better, imagine a 4x4 off-roader type vehicle – you know, the type hunters and farmers drive around in – with the windows down and turbo-folk music blaring out with this guy driving like there's a prize if he loses me following behind. As we got closer to the destination, I started getting familiar with my surroundings, and I could tell we were approaching the airport. It was one of those moments of mine where I'd lost all sense of judgement and I just had to go with it and wait and see what the outcome would be.

We parked up, walked towards the airport, then walked

past it. 'Hey, the airport,' I said.

'No, this way,' he replied.

We walked to a building next to the airport and upon entry passed security, emptied our pockets, scanned etc., and as we walked further into the building, it transformed into a dome with an open end. I could see it, there it was, in all its glory: a Cessna private jet.

'Wow!' I exclaimed in complete awe of the plane. What seemed tiny in the distance, sort of like a small toy plane, started to become to grander as I got closer. It was the first ever time I had witnessed a private jet in real life. The steps were laid out ready to board, and as I looked around there was just the runway and this plane. This was the first real taste I had of what it must be like to live a life of luxury. I've got to admit, my personality tends to get bored of gimmicks pretty quickly, but of course, this was far from a gimmick.

I entered the plane and looked around. It was everything you'd expect it to be: walnut finish, hand-sewn leather upholstery – it was out of this world.

As I left the plane and my feet touched the ground again, I was back in my own shoes, but for those five to ten minutes on board that plane I was 'living the dream' some may say!

'So you want it?' asked the chap who secured the plane. 'Yeah, it'll do,' I said.

And within two days we were using this magnificent private jet to shoot a music video with. What I quickly started to learn working out in Eastern Europe was that nothing can be judged at face value, and you'd be a fool to think it could.

There I was on home soil having delivered yet another boundary-pushing, never-before-seen-in-this-part-of-the-world video. I needed to secure further work, so I got talking to the artist about his plans. It turned out that he'd only gone and launched his own record label! You know that feeling when you've achieved something, like a run outside, or an intense workout, then you take that breath and you pause, you can feel your blood circulate around your body and something sinks in, deep inside your stomach? That was the feeling I had of 'I nailed it!'

I negotiated a rate to do all of the artist's music videos, and there were about 12 artists to start with. Songs were coming in thick and fast, and at this point you needed to maintain the level of creativity, but to handle it all you needed a team so that you can focus on steering the ship. The music video game just went up a notch; well, it seemed to work more like a factory for me!

By the time I had wrapped up a contract with the record label to film all their artists' music videos, put things in place, see a few projects through, I sold the company.

I was feeling a little empty at this stage. I was getting closer to 30, and success to me was a yacht – one that I actually own. I didn't have my own yacht and let's just say I wasn't surrounded by good people; they were all superficial.

I felt flat with a huge sense of underachievement. The whole journey in showbiz was tiring, but at this point I'm doubting myself big time.

'Am I a businessman?' I thought to myself. 'Do I even know what I'm doing?' It was time to start another chapter in my life and get a job!

CHAPTER 6

The Monopoly man

With all the doubt going on in my mind and no idea what I wanted to do next, I started looking into employment at 29 years old! The last time I was employed I was 17 and a head barman (glorified glass collector) at The Hilton! How do I start? Where do I look? What do I do?

Well, LinkedIn was the answer, and I started to scroll endlessly, looking for something that made sense. All of these job titles were alien to me! I really didn't know where to start or what to do, cliché as it sounds, until one day I scrolled past one job which caught my interest.

It read, 'You will develop Monopoly games' – I thought to myself, 'That's what I want!'

There I am in central London parking up a car which is worth more than the annual salary, ready to walk into an interview for the first time in 10 years. Out of my comfort zone again, off I went not knowing what to expect and what I was getting myself in for.

A famous red door in Paddington may get some into trouble, but for me, it symbolised Christmas. I guess that was down to the Monopoly games in my mind. I opened the door and in the hallway entrance was this beautiful figure of a lion to impersonate a Monopoly playing piece with Monopoly money and illustrations all over it. The walls were framed with various board games. I felt right at home, it was a warm feeling of security being in a place that felt familiar, and knowing how friendly the toy trade was, I predicted that this was going to be good.

I arrived at reception and in no time I was in the meeting room. A fairly smart young chap walks in – polite, well spoken, he had Cambridge written all over him, and we clicked. We talked on end about the industry, toys, board games, my experiences ... and I landed the job and suddenly I'm a director!

Panic! What do I do now! Does this mean I cannot be me anymore?

For my first few days I wrote a journal of what I was doing: 09:00 sent email, 09:05 phone call. I was completely lost; it was here that I learnt how tough I had been on myself over the years. All of this self-criticising wasn't good; I'd look at how I spent my time literally by the hour and if it wasn't productive, I wasn't happy! It was at this company that I learnt that it wasn't about the number of hours you sit at a desk, or typing up whatever – it was all about results. This was a shock for me because my train of thought was, if you could achieve that in one hour, then do it 10 times a day! Clearly that wasn't the direction here, it was all about strategy and results. Anyway, as time went on, I started to 'fit in' – in fact I bought a whole new wardrobe to help me blend in – and I just generally started to enjoy life. Being able to 'switch off' was something I was never able to do, but all of a sudden, I had hours of time that I could use on myself! Wow!

So this company specialised in board games. They had the licence to games like Monopoly and owned a few of their own well-known brands too. My job was to grow their business in parts of the world where they had no business at all. For me this was the ultimate test to see whether I was 'good' and cut out to be in business or not.

The first call I made to a Serbian business selling toys I will never forget. I called them up, explained who I was, what I was doing and what I was selling. The first thing these guys said to me was 'Good luck. People haven't got money to eat food out here, let alone play games that are as expensive as that.' Now, believe me when I tell you that those words in Serbian hit my heart like a dagger. There's something about the Serbian language that can be so graphic, spiteful and hurtful, all delivered in a throwaway kind of attitude that can really take a lot out of you if you're not used to it. It's Eastern Europe and these guys are thick-skinned! So I put down the phone, feeling deflated … then I went at it again, this time with someone on the other end of the phone that knew what I was talking about. Then the next call, a success too, I'm off! And where did I find these people? Google! It was that simple. I was by no means an international toy trade expert, but I soon figured out who I'd need to talk to.

I've got to admit the best thing about this job was I was my own boss. I could do what I want (within reason) as long as the results were delivered. This was where I learnt about the real values of trust within business. My businesses prior to this role never grew to over 100 staff that were managed by me. My model would always be to outsource tasks where possible, as opposed to taking on risks of employing people at a start-up stage for special projects. As soon as those projects became regular and the skill set was needed, that's when I'd employ. Of course, this comes with a consequence which was I'd never 'let go' of 'holding the bull by its horns'. This meant that most times I was completely immersed into most things. In my current role, the trust was there for me to plan, attack and deliver – this wasn't company terminology, but more of my mindset on delivery.

The first project I had was to create a Serbian edition of Monopoly – this was going to be so cool! When I had the toy shops, we'd all get together and play Monopoly every so often, and I cannot explain how much I love the game. It's worth mentioning I used to always win at Monopoly – I won't give away my secret, but it doesn't involve me being the banker each time.

I felt like I had won a prize in a gameshow. I was off to create my own edition of Monopoly, but the Serbian version. Where do I start? What do I do? How do I do it?

As the drawing board was a place where I spent a lot of time, I understood that everyone who plays Monopoly loves the editions to be personal and that they'd connect with the property squares on an emotional basis. So my research had begun, and I was out to find the best spots in Serbia that could fill this Monopoly board-to-be.

My flight was booked, my plan of action was in place and I'd become a travelling salesman ready to build a board game empire in the Balkans. There I was in Belgrade, unpacking my suitcase, ready to take the country by storm with a press conference in the morning. My phone was ringing constantly with officials and delegates who were also attending the press conference to ask a few questions as they were just as excited as I was. And that's when it kicked in: I realised I was proud of what I was doing, even though the brand was a 'children's game'. At some social events in the past when I owned the toy stores, I felt a little uncomfortable saying what I actually did. The conversation would go around the table and it'd be 'I'm in finance,' 'I'm in insurance,' 'I'm in IT,' 'I'm in property,' then I'd tell them that I owned toy shops. It was almost like it was not a serious business, so I'd shy away from mentioning it – even though the industry is worth £3 billion. All of a sudden, however, I was known to many as the Monopoly man, and boy, I was not shy about that!

As I walked into the city hall with chairs laid out and a panel at the top, with cameramen and journalists setting up, you'd think I was about to deliver 'new lockdown rules' during a pandemic – the tone of the whole vibe was something else. I managed to get the country so excited about their edition of Monopoly and at that point I realised why that was – because of me!

They say that laughter is the most contagious thing in the world, although personally I'd like to rephrase it: laughter is the most contagious thing in the world that's positive! Well, so is passion, and I was able to pick up the phone before my trip to Belgrade and talk to people in different sectors from tourism, banking and hospitality, and I was able to share my passion about this project, so much so that these official dignitaries were lining up ready to declare that the country was about to receive a wonderful symbolic product.

The cameras were rolling, there was a live feed to a national broadcaster, and I was ready not to screw anything up. It was the first time I was about to be on live TV and the focus was on me. I remember gulping on water but my mouth being constantly dry. 'Oh no,' I thought. 'Ignore it, ignore it.'

The conference opened and as I was about to speak. My microphone was turned on and I was the most serious Monopoly man you could ever think of. I think that I psyched myself out so much that I was petrified. Also, this terrible voice in my head kept saying, 'You've screwed it up, you don't say that word like that.' That horrible voice of doubt was picking on anything negative it could find. So you could say I felt uneasy talking in a second language in front of an audience on live TV, but I did it – and nope, I didn't screw up!

After the conference, I went around the country talking about partnerships and projects going forward. It was the kickstart that was needed for such a large project with so many eyeballs on the game! One theory about negotiation is that every country, every city even, has its own way of doing business. On my trip I was joined by a colleague. He too was enthusiastic about his role but also a little oblivious to what some people were actually saying. We were negotiating a partnership with a company, and they were interested, but they needed time to think. So the chap I'm with decided to push the sale, even though the guy on the receiving end was twice our size and weight and had been chewing a wasp throughout the whole interview. He was a mean dude and was no-nonsense when it came to commercial deals.

'Well, it's just going to be great, it's a once-in-a-lifetime opportunity,' said my colleague.

We all looked at the mean dude in anticipation of a reply. The silence began to become deafening.

He lifted chin slowly.

He reached for tie and gave it a firm pull. He gritted his teeth slowly and loudly.

'I said, I'll be in touch.'

'Yep, yep, sure,' said my colleague. He got the message; he'd pushed a little too far.

Now, an important part of negotiating is that you don't push – well, at least not in that part of the world. If they want something, they want it. These are hard-nosed Europeans that have been through a lot and really have that cold, straight face which the best comedian would find it tough to crack a smile from. What I'm saying is, negotiation is a two-way thing, so you've got to be able to navigate the situation and you've both got to win. Nobody wants to be on the bad end of a deal. The game launched some six months later and was a fantastic success, with a red-carpet ceremony fit for a presidential launch. The president never turned up, but all those dignitaries that were high up did, and just like that, Monopoly Serbia was launched!

Oh, and me being me, it wasn't just Serbia I was doing, it was Montenegro too – at the same time, parallel to this project. Why? Well, I guess it's back to that deep-end scenario: you've got to jump in the deep end and make it work if you want big results!

Over a short space of time, the business grew, and I started to get noticed. At this point the CEO was taking time out to spend with me and giving me 'nuggets'. These weren't from a Happy Meal; these were business nuggets that he'd kept hidden away, not fully developed. Almost like an intro, it was up to you to go in and make the deal work.

The very first opportunity I had to create a big deal, I did, and I hit the ball out of the park. There appeared to be an opportunity for a global petrol station to create their own promotion using aspects of our brand, with all the hurdles you could possibly think of in the way. But all in all, it worked out as one of the biggest deals in the company's history, and a few years later I repeated it and bagged another!

Russia was seen as the land of opportunities but also a very grey area for the company. They had an employee who lived in Moscow and attempted to trade, but he didn't cut it and delivered a big fat zero. After growing existing markets, I looked to Russia and it was my next target. I know how to converse a little in Russian; or rather, I just talk Serbian with a twist in the hope that the person I'm talking to is listening carefully enough to understand. I had a map of countries I was conquering and there was Russia, the largest country by land mass about to become the new home for a lot of product.

I was lucky that I had that advantage of understanding the country and people to an extent that I could converse with them. One of my most memorable moments was the first trade deal in Russia. Now, this wasn't textbook stuff, this was more like something straight from a sitcom. I had sent out a few offers and I received an interesting reply with an appetite for trade. Fantastic! I sensed a deal and got to work.

A call was arranged between me and this particular distributor, and before the call I did my research and looked for a profile of the person I'd be speaking to, but nope, I couldn't find anybody from Russia with that name. The only person I found was some kid probably from Dubai; surely it couldn't be him, he barely looked 20 years old. The call started and we introduced each other and our businesses. I noticed that the pitch of the voice was quite high. Can it be? Surely not! So I asked what it was like in Moscow? 'Oh it's very nice, but cold,' he said. 'Yes, I'd rather live in Dubai than Moscow,' I said.

'I studied in Dubai,' he said. 'Oh, really?' (Gotcha!)

As our conversation progressed and we talked numbers and forecasts, I realised I was dealing with a boardgame genius who had a world-class ranking in chess, and his company were also distributing another UK brand in Russia. So I decided to be bold and call him out:

'Look, the offer you've sent us is something I'd expect from an 18-year-old kid who has no idea what he's doing in this industry. We can get a trade deal in place with your company, but the other interested parties are paying at least 40% more than your offer. It's great what you're doing with the other brand, but we need someone serious for our outfit.'

'Leave it with me, I'll call you back,' he replied.

And so, he did, and the deal was done with the Russian company. It turned out him and his dad ran a highly successful board game business, with this genius knowing the market inside out! I pumped up the numbers a little and called him out to an extent, and it worked. It seemed that his weakness of concealing his age not to be perceived as a young guy who doesn't know what he was doing hurt him, and the deal was based on ego rather than economics.

The largest toy fair in Europe is held each year in a city

called Nuremberg where all the trade suppliers meet. This Russian company came along to meet us, and the secret was out. It goes to show that you must understand what your potential weakness could be when in business and conceal or eliminate it out of the equation so it's not used against you. In this case the chap didn't want to be perceived as a novice with no idea of what he was doing, so he wasn't letting on that he'd just finished university and that this was his first business! Credit where it's due, but by the time we met with his father it was a different story all together. His father was a trader to the bone; he would give you a sob story that would make his enemy pity him, then walk away with the upper end of the deal. I could see his son was embarrassed slightly by his style, but he also respected it as it worked.

Greece, Serbia, Russia, Norway and a lot more of these countries which started out with zero were turning over handsome numbers. After five years and millions of pounds in revenue secured and more deals in the pipeline, it was time for me to move on. I patted myself on the back and knew it was time to part.

To be fair, after the first two years I was ready to go, but I wanted to 'stick at it', as I wanted to be more disciplined and not jump ship as I thought it was a bad trait. As it turns out, it's not; you've got to go with your instinct. Having said that, you've got to think these decisions through and not just rush to the next 'big opportunity'.

So, I built a division that would last, passed the business on and was off to seek more opportunities.

But what did I have in mind? What would I do next? This time I had a plan!

Side activities

So, you're employed, used to having the freedom to do what you want, but now you've got the freedom of switching off, which you never had before. It seemed like you had idle hours. I never mentioned that my commute was a four-hour daily commute. So I had time to play with, and I couldn't use train time to kill hours, I had to be productive. It's important to point out that while I was employed, I never had a side-hustle, another way to earn an income, and the reason was that I didn't want the employer to feel he had been cheated, that my efforts on making money were going elsewhere. While that's all changed today in the business landscape, and it's seen as OK to do so, I just felt a little unethical about it, so I never did it.

What I did do, however, was look into pro-bono roles and see what it was I could do to give back to the community in some way, shape or form. I found an opening to be a candidate for a UK & Ireland Delegate to the Serbian Diaspora Assembly. I liked the sound of it, enquired about it and off the application went to the Round Table. A few weeks passed and then I was elected.

I'd spend a lot of time at various meetings discussing the Serbian activity in the UK, whether that be from a community point of view or planning activities, and I seemed to be putting in hours into something that I loved. It was further keeping me connected to the Serbs in the UK and also in Serbia.

The problem was that I was elected as a UK & IRE delegate to the assembly of Serbia, which had been defunct for a number of years, so although you were representing the community and organisations, you never had that central forum to meet with the other representatives around the world and exchange information. However, by taking on the role I would actively look at ways to implement new practices in engaging the community nationwide and also bridging the two countries.

I guess by showing my eagerness, I attracted interest from the Serbian Council of Great Britain who approached me to become a board member and help develop their activities. Before I knew it I had signed away any glimpse of free time I thought I had and was knee deep in creating blueprints for non-profits on growth.

The Serbian Council of Great Britain is an apolitical organisation that's non-profit and its interest is to promote the work of the Serbian community in GB. Now going into this organisation all seemed a bit grey, as in how do you measure that? What are the deliverables? Upon learning about the individuals behind the scenes and their common passion, I shared their values exactly. Now that's important, to surround yourself with people who share the same ideologies and principles. You may not be like-minded in the sense that you don't all agree on everything, but being part of a team that shares the same direction is so important, especially when you are doing it on a pro-bono basis – otherwise you'll just walk!

The first task was to breathe some life into the organisation, bring some creativity and activity that the committee hadn't seen before. I looked at the structure and figured out what I could bring to the table, and that was exactly it: a fresh approach to pretty much everything. Given what we have experienced in 2020 from virtual meetings to virtual concerts, everything was new for the committee, and it was a steep learning curve.

When joining the board, I never thought I'd make long-lasting connections and friends. That's another part of business/non-profits that you don't actually think about. Meeting new people all over the world, hearing new stories, learning about new developments – you are always up to date, but most of all you are communicating, which is what we all love to do as humans.

Another role I have taken on is trustee of the Serbian Orthodox Church, which is very close to my heart as my father was instrumental in the purchase of the property and also the building of the new church, which is only the second purpose-built Serbian Orthodox Church in the UK. This role keeps me close to the local Serbian community and in touch with the people I grew up with. It also reminds me of the days I'd help my father around the Church for services and how the community used to be when it was thriving.

My initial worry when taking on an employment role was that sense of freedom you have when you are an entrepreneur. As I mentioned earlier, my mindset was always: if you have a job, that's it, you can't do anything else – which was always alien to me. But I fed my hunger to learn and grow through joining pro-bono organisations which wouldn't detract from my commercial interest of my 'job' but would supplement my learning and all-round growth.

If you're feeling flat in your career, a pro-bono role is something that can really propel your mindset and feed that hunger from elsewhere. Another job may not be the answer, and it may be a problem to seek it. I'd 100% recommend a pro-bono additional role if your time allows you to.

With any pro-bono role it is essentially that you're passionate about what you are doing. You're not doing a paid role, so making that effort to be at a meeting, event or helping out in any way you can doesn't have a financial incentive. So you walk away from that activity with a 'feel good factor' that money can't buy. Whether you are innovating the way your community recycles or putting plans in place for a new ecosystem, it's all got to be done with passion.

For anybody thinking about taking up a pro-bono role, don't forget that it's not the time you put in, but it's the outcome of what you can achieve that counts. However, if you're looking at a pro-bono role for status/self-gratification, then the role isn't for you. People in these circles are generally quick to sniff out self-gratifiers or self-publicising narcissists.

I've dealt with them in the past and seen them being dealt with, and let me tell you, it's not pretty.

So, if you're reading this book and looking at ways of self-promotion, then put the book down and give it to someone who has a real interest in helping others around them – this book isn't for you.

Humanity, royalty & world leaders

During the days of the toy store and showbiz in 2014, there were disastrous floods that took place in Serbia. It was so bad that it wiped out the town of Obrenovac, and witnessing this on the news reminded me of my childhood. It was one of those moments when you're witnessing something so catastrophic yet you feel helpless in that there is not much you can do.

The human instinct is to help. I had seen this first-hand from my late mother, and it was a reaction that didn't take much thought at all. I knew I had to help, and I'd do whatever I possibly could to help those in need.

Now, let me tell you to what extent my late mother would help out. Each holiday she took the largest suitcase you could imagine and filled it with clothes, cosmetics and gifts to hand out to family and those in need that had just escaped the war and packed as little as possible for herself. We once arrived in Belgrade and this suitcase was strapped to the top of a car our grandad was driving. Now, this car was a Lada for anybody who knows what that is. It's the iconic look of Eastern Europe in the nineties. We were driving along when I noticed a reflection every so often to my side. We stop at traffic lights and I see this reflection – it's us in a shop window. The suitcase strapped to the top of the car was almost the same length as the car itself! I couldn't believe it! Jokes aside, the first things my mother would always pack would be clothes and gifts for the family and friends. In the UK she would pack parcels and send them home to help. There really was no end to her humanitarian heart.

My first move was to secure transport. I wanted to send a truck of aid in less than a week; that was the goal I set. Calling around various people, I stumbled across a logistics agent who deals in Serbia and happened to have a truck leaving the UK pretty soon for Serbia 'empty'! Off I went, calling around, getting people and companies to donate aid.

News travelled and the next day a priest from Halifax drove a Luton van down with two other chaps to the warehouse full of aid to be sent. The warehouse was turned into an aid centre literally overnight with people working tirelessly, sorting packages out and putting things together. It was really wonderful to see people get together for a common goal – to help those in need!

Over this short period of time, hundreds of people were in

and out of the warehouse, from all over the UK, all bringing in their donations. I took it one step further and decided to reach out to local businesses, all of whom were very generous donating everything from bacterial wipes to water.

At one point the Serbian Embassy called me up and asked if they could send some of their aid, as the national carrier can only take four tonnes a day on their flight from Heathrow to Belgrade.

Within 10 days, 24 tonnes of aid was on its way to Serbia to help those that needed it most. But we didn't stop there. I managed to find a young man who became an internet sensation playing the accordion with a twist. He'd play global hits on an accordion; the songs were gimmicky but cool! He flew over from Italy, stayed with us and we raised a few thousand pounds to send to Serbia along with the aid.

Now, the whole point of providing aid was for everybody to dig in and help out. Sure, you can send money or buy a truck of filled with water/nappies etc. But for one, that's rare and two, you want the whole community to get together and create movement, and that's exactly what was achieved. From fundraising in local supermarkets, to whip-rounds at work to raise money, it was all a collective effort that we hope made a difference.

Also, you'll always have one or more idiots who know it all and achieve nothing at the end of it. You know those cartoons where you have the bad guy who's only out to mess things up, that's their only intention. Well, I found out a long time ago that they're not only in cartoons and that these idiots take up oxygen on earth too. You know the type, the ones that will make up ridiculous lies for their own satisfaction of trying to piss on your parade. In my time I've come across a lot of these, all of whom I feel sorry for. They're spending too much time worrying about you and looking at your life instead of spending time making their life better.

One day I get a call asking me, 'Are you sending aid to Serbia?' 'Yeah, of course I am,' I said.

'Well, 'idiot x' just called me up and said they're driving a van down to the Embassy to hand over aid as it goes directly to Serbia, and apparently, you're sending the aid to your own shop? But don't tell them I told you this,' they say.

'In that case you're better to send the aid directly to the Embassy,' I said.

Two days later, the same person calls me up.

'They drove the aid to the Embassy and the staff there told them that they're working with you, sending stuff from the Embassy, and why take a 100-mile trip when someone in Corby is collecting aid.' I laugh and hang up.

These idiots turn up to the warehouse not knowing where to look and hand over aid. What do you do? You ignore them, but you also laugh as you show recognition that you know what they're about.

I'm an advocate of the truth and sooner or later the truth always appears. But I decided to fly out to Belgrade and wait for the truck to appear to the Red Cross and prove to any doubters that the aid had in fact arrived at its destination and not to some imaginary shop!

What I learnt was, we are all human at the end of the day, but humanity is helping those that are in need without anything in return, and that in itself is beautiful. Little did I know that experiencing this first-hand would ignite a flame in my heart that later in life would continue to burn and it would inspire me to help those in need more.

These were the days when social media wasn't so big, you weren't posting what you had for lunch. When I see people helping those in need now, then recording themselves, it doesn't look good. Don't do it for self-gratification or to show others that you've just given a homeless person some money. Sit down with them and talk, learn about what it is that got them there, find out if they want help.

Mental health is one of the most complex subjects that is unique to each individual; there isn't a right or a blanket answer for all. The best commodity we have is time, and if you are able to spend that time with someone who needs it, you've given the biggest gift of all.

The royal call

I never really used to believe in those 'it just happened' stories until I started to experience them for myself. You know the type of stories that you hear: 'I was just chatting to x, y, z and we came up with an idea for this,' and all of sudden it's a success. Well, that's what I'm talking about, those encounters and those conversations that can turn into something BIG.

After a business trip in Athens I was headed for more business meetings in Belgrade. At Athens International Airport at check-in I saw somebody I recognised, but as it was quite a distance away and I didn't want to be as rude as I usually am and stare/squint to try and make out who it was, I didn't say anything.

Most flights I spend writing down notes or on my laptop, unless I'm completely exhausted, in which case I'd be out for the count. By the time I landed in Belgrade, I'd forgotten about that familiar face I'd seen at check-in until I got to the luggage conveyor belt and I looked up and saw His Royal Highness Crown Prince Alexander of Serbia with his wife, Her Royal Highness Crown Princess Katherine of Serbia. At this point I felt butterflies in my stomach; I remembered them both from my childhood when they lived in the UK and would attend various church gatherings. They would speak with my mother and father, but I hadn't seen them in a long time; the last time I'd seen them I must have been 9 years old.

Now do I remember this moment and when I get home, say, 'Guess who I saw?'

Or do I smile politely from a distance respectfully in acknowledgement that I know who they are and greet them with a nod.

No, I couldn't do that. Who knows if I'd ever see them again or have the opportunity to talk to them!

I had to go over and talk to them. On my approach, these two large men out of nowhere stepped forward. There seemed to be a signal that I was 'OK' and so I said, 'Hello.'

This would be one 'hello' I would never forget for the rest of my life.

As we spoke, we joined the dots of my family, upbringing and how we met while I was a child. HRH Crown Princess Katherine asked me if I could assist in an upcoming event that her charity would be running in London the following month at the University Women's Club in Mayfair.

My inner child giggled and said, 'Hold on, you're talking to a princess and the princess is asking you to help out? You've got to be kidding me!'

'Yes, it would be my pleasure,' I say. I mean, after all, how could you turn down an offer like that!

We exchanged contacts and to my surprise HRH Crown Princess Katherine was on the case, emailing me introductions to her foundation at the Royal Palace in Belgrade. All of a sudden, I was being overwhelmed with information. But as you know by now, that's what I thrive on!

Within a short space of time I was immersed in the activity of HRH, her charities around the world and how she'd been helping Serbia for over 25 years, fundraising millions of pounds of aid and equipment to better the healthcare in the country. All of this from a princess who is of Greek origin but has taken the Serbian people to her heart and loves the children like they are her own.

Over time I was introduced to the board members of Lifeline Humanitarian Organisation in the UK who are a husband-and-wife team that have been on the board since inception. These two are the most incredible people that you could ever meet, completely selfless and with a passion for helping out HRH's mission. I met with them and discussed plans about how to boost activity and ideas for the charity. Following the meeting I presented the plans discussed and all was 'full steam ahead' from there.

Before I knew it, the following year, I was a board member and organising the 25th anniversary gala dinner at Claridge's in London – one of the most prestigious hotels in the world. For those of who you don't know, Claridge's is one of London's most iconic hotels, situated in Mayfair. Not only that, but HRH Crown Prince Alexander was born in Claridge's in July, 1945. Then, Yugoslavia in 1941 was under attack in World War Two, King Peter II left the country to live in exile in London. King Peter II and his wife Queen Alexandra then took up residence in Claridge's.

Now, to be royal you had to be born on home soil, so suite 212 of Claridge's where the Yugoslav royal family resided became Yugoslavia for 24 hours, with thanks to Winston Churchill who allowed this. The Patriarch of Yugoslavia brought soil from Yugoslavia and placed it under the bed, and the future King of Yugoslavia was born!

I don't know about you, but just the weight of that story to me is overwhelming. Imagine now putting all of that history into perspective and realising you were responsible for making the 25th anniversary gala dinner a success, in the same hotel where all of this happened?

'Stop the ride, I want to get off!' That probably went through my mind, but like anything you do, if you put your name to it, own it and deliver it. Nobody likes empty promises or somebody that doesn't deliver; the only thing that's stopping you from making it a success is you.

After a few pep talks to myself, I was ready for it. Having the invitations designed, approved, collecting the print, posting them out, dealing with RSVPs I was totally in immersive mode. I was in, the event had my full focus. It had to be a success; it was a milestone celebration that had to make an impact!

Budgeting the evening, tickets, costs – the whole thing just felt like there was a lot more pressure than other projects I'd been involved with. Regardless of the total revenue, it was a very high-profile event and one where you just couldn't slip up at all!

One day I received a message from HRH saying I should contact a person she had recently met. It turned out that this gentleman was in the events industry and was willing to help make the event look as it should – premium – with his teams' capabilities. Now as anybody owning a budget, the first question is, how much is it going to cost? 'Nothing,' he said. 'I'm helping from my heart'. It's those conversations that you have with people that hit home and you feel good. You feel good because you realise there are good people out there and they genuinely want to help. I found out over time that this gentleman and I would become good friends, and it's down to that formula of having people around you who share the same ideology that provides the common ground for any friendship. After days and weeks of planning, meeting and organising everything from what food should be served to the table arrangements and the lighting colour, it was the night of the anniversary gala and everybody was excited. We had over 200 people attending, from Serbia's Minister of Health to the Ambassador of Kuwait. I was feeling slightly nervous, but I was more excited than anything.

The evening turned out to be a huge success. Everybody who attended had a great time, the evening was full of entertainment, from traditional folklore dancing to ballroom dancing, an auction by Sotheby's, a solo violinist and speeches from Their Royal Highnesses. We raised over £30,000 in one evening with promises of further donations to follow soon after.

Following the gala dinner, I visited Serbia to deliver the medical equipment purchased, which was an ultrasound machine to the general hospital of Čačak in Serbia. I was honoured to share the journey with HRH to the hospital to deliver the ultrasound machine. During this journey I was left astonished at how HRH never seems to stop working. She would spend hours talking to people in New York, Canada and Greece about various different projects around Serbia and the need for help for specific equipment, from hospital beds, defibrillators, incubators and more.

Most people, including me, would think that a princess would be shielded from talking to various people and have teams working for her. There's one thing about HRH Crown Princess Katherine that you cannot find, replicate or see anywhere else, and that is the size of her heart. The tireless work she puts in so that the people in the country can receive better healthcare is truly out of this world. It was at this point of our journey that I realised that I'll never be able to meet someone like HRH ever again. These are the kind of people that you read about or see on TV, the kind that devote their whole life to a cause.

We arrived at the general hospital of Čačak to meet the mayor and the director of the hospital. We discussed the equipment that was being delivered, and to my surprise this was the first ultrasound machine the hospital had ever had. The staff and professionals were so happy to have such equipment to make their jobs better. Can you imagine going to work without the tools you need? Without Wi-Fi? Or a laptop or smartphone? Well, these doctors were doing just that. They were working without the right tools and yet they were still helping to improve the health of their patients. But to see their pleasure of having such equipment, which will make scans more visible, sharp and detailed so that they can analyse patients much more effectively, was an eye-opener.

After our meeting, a short press conference was held, and

HRH met the patients of the hospital and talked with them about their health, treatment and learnt about what they were going through. Following that we had a meeting with all the nurses and doctors, and the princess said loudly: 'What else do you need?'

There was silence.

'If you don't tell me what you need, how can I help?' she asked. Further silence.

'There is no shame in asking for help,' she added.

'A car to transport chemotherapy patients,' a nurse replied. 'A lot of patients during chemotherapy are too weak to take public transport and cannot travel for treatment. If we have a car we can transport them for their treatment,' the nurse added.

'You'll have a car next week' said the princess. 'What else is needed? Please tell me,' she added.

'We need more hospital beds,' said a doctor.

'We've got a container coming in 10 days. How many beds do you need?' the princess asked.

The head of the foundation discussed beds and other equipment with the doctor and took notes on his notepad. The hospital visit then concluded, and we travelled back to Belgrade.

'Lazar, we promised the hospital a car and we need to deliver a car next week,' HRH said to me. 'Let's get working on delivering that car,' she added.

On the journey home, myself and HRH made telephone calls to find donors for the hospital. By the time we got back to the palace, a car had been secured. The following week, HRH called me to say the cars had been delivered.

I've met a lot of successful people in life, and the most common thing they all have in common is their determination. The determination to succeed and the hunger to deliver. To me these traits really set apart those who are mediocre and those who are highly successful.

Now, if anybody had told me that I'd be running a London office for a royal charity, there's no way I'd have believed them. It goes to show you that anything can happen in life, but it's you that needs to make it happen. It may be a sign, a coincidence or even an accident, but there's always something positive to be gained out of any experience. It's your job to find out what it is and go for it.

Meeting people that are happy with their job is like meeting the happiest people on the planet. Many people lose their purpose in life searching for something they love and letting so many opportunities go by without noticing. If you can find that job or even that cause that makes you happy or helps you fill that void you may feel inside, then you are blessed. I find that those people who are happy in their work are those who are happy at home too. For some people it may take a while to find it, but once you've found it, a whole new dimension opens.

Advising world leaders

I guess those of you reading this who know me are thinking, yep, I've seen his social media posts and I know exactly who he's advising. Well, you may be wrong, simply for the fact that although it may seem that I post 'everything' on social media, in fact, I don't actually. A lot of things that are of a personal nature or require confidentiality will never make their way on those kinds of platforms.

Now can you imagine what it must feel like to be brought up with such an open mind that you really believe deep down inside yourself that you can make a change, you can make things happen! Then you start doing it, and it snowballs, and more opportunities arise, you create more opportunities and so on and so forth. Well believe me, like anything, once you start running, you get better at it – quicker, leaner, stronger.

Over the past 10 years I've been so fortunate to be able to meet people from all over the world and with many different backgrounds, mainly because I'd push myself to the front of the queue and be there, at those places, exactly where you'd expect to find them. There's no use in sending smoke signals to someone who never goes outside and no point in sending letters to someone who doesn't read, so my logic has always been simple. Meet the decision maker or person in charge, present your opportunity and allow them to get back to you. It really is that simple. Now, planning and presenting the opportunity is equally the hardest part and I'll talk about that a little later. But just as important is your presentation and to know the subject matter about what you are talking about.

I've met diplomats, ambassadors and world leaders over time, and it'll always be flattering when you're asked to advise on certain sectors. It hasn't happened a lot, I've got to admit, but it has happened more than once and each and every time, the inner child awakes: 'Get – Outta – Here!'

Can you imagine that those people who told me 'you can't do that or say 'do one thing at a time' never get the opportunity to meet the calibre of people that I'm meeting and be placed in front of a world leader who's asking you for your view, your opinion and your advice on a subject matter. I'd say that's a pretty big deal – I'd also say it means that if you want to spread your wings and explore the world, then you go and do it!

Now, I don't want to go into too much detail here as I don't see myself as politically astute. At the moment, I'm not into politics, but as time goes on you never know if that will change. I'd confidently say that I'm apolitical as my mindset is dominantly commercial at present, and where I can help anyone out with my advice on the latest trends, start-ups and investment I'd always gladly talk to them.

However, what I've learnt is that I have the ability to grow businesses, and I've proven that this can be applied to a number of things. So, if region 'x' wants to learn how to attract tourism, I can help. If they want to learn how to make their IT sector more attractive, I can help with that too – the list goes on.

The key for most people doing business in other countries

is incentives: what is it that sets your country apart from the others? Is it the low tax rate? Proximity to Europe/London/US? The natural beauty of the country? Currency? There are a lot of factors to consider when you're trying to bring, move and invest trade into a new country.

But I don't want to bore you with that kind of stuff. I want you to know that you can be that person who hasn't had a Harvard, Cambridge or Oxford education but who has real-life experiences that they can share to make someone who has a lot of authority make a more educated decision when faced with that task. It doesn't matter about your background, the last job you had or the one you have now. It doesn't even matter if you don't have a job now. What matters is your experience, your story. If you are able to share your advice with someone or an organisation on a matter that is difficult to tackle, then you too are helping out by sharing that advice.

What I want you to be able to take away is that the traditional path that would lead you to a goal is not the only way you can achieve it. It's been proven by so many, especially recently; you have had people like Trump, who has never been a politician, become one of the world's most powerful leaders, and he wasn't educated in political studies either. Maybe Trump's a bad example for some, but let's just say, don't pigeonhole yourself if you feel that you can offer the world more!

CHAPTER

8

Know what you want

I've always liked the idea of owning several businesses, each in different sectors. You'll meet people that will say, 'You can't be a jack of all trades' or 'Focus on one thing' – that's all valid. But it's your life and your destiny, so while you listen to some people giving you their advice, you need to know deep down inside what you want to do, and then go and do it!

For me, being 'dynamic' is what I've learnt over time is what keeps me interested and on my toes. I guess some would call me a serial entrepreneur (among many other things, of course!) as I can't sit still and I'm always working on something! After leaving my role as the Monopoly man, I decided it was time to grow an empire, but of course I had an idea of the areas I wanted to be involved in.

I Love Digital

One of the many things I've learnt about myself is that, like all of us, I have unique skills and can be very creative. My principles in all my businesses were twofold: sales and marketing. You need to be able to sell but you also need to communicate effectively what you're selling. So, what I decided to do was form a digital marketing agency. The idea of the agency was that it was to be a boutique agency focusing on a select number of clients. The reason for that was simple: you'd have 'immersion' and 'results', looking after everything from web development through to content and social media management. Like any start-up, you need clients or sales, and I knew people who needed various marketing services. So, I started talking to them about winning business.

The questions that were extremely important for me to ask myself were: Where do I pitch this agency? Who is my target? What price do I charge? After all, I was building a business. A friend of mine owns a very large company in the UK with hundreds of stores. So I approached him with some marketing ideas and said what we could offer. He liked the idea and signed off some TV commercials. There it was, our first contract.

All of a sudden, I heard that inner child of mine again. This time he said, 'Are you kidding me? You? TV commercials for a national chain? Get out of here!'

At the drop of a hat I had assembled a team, the shoot, storyboard and locations. It really was that easy, all because of the previous experience I had of doing it. That's the secret to easy business: know what you're doing. If you don't know what you're doing, hire someone who does!

We shot around six TVCs for the client and they were very impressed with it. Not only was it high end stuff but it fitted within their budget too. The first project was complete, and it ticked a lot of boxes.

Now, let me tell you about my friend. He is the type of guy that you can 'smell money from'. Now he doesn't just wear labels or 'in your face', 'look at me' sort of attire, but the way he holds himself and discusses things, you can sense the confidence and also the sharp attitude that he has; it's tough to explain. But I guess once you know who he is, then it all falls into place.

There's one trait I love about this guy which makes him a great character. If we're out, for example, he'll never shy away from offering to pay for anything and always insists, which we battle over frequently.

But when it comes to business, he'll hammer away and nail you down to win, each and every time – not in a nasty way, but in the ethical way of how the company operates. It's all hierarchical: buy cheap, sell cheap.

If you're driving a Bentley, you wouldn't think twice about fitting the most expensive tyres. However, if you're driving a car on its last legs that had just scraped through its MOT, why would you go and spend a fortune on a paint job? You just wouldn't. Well, that's him, all relative, and he's quick to adapt to any situation that is thrown at him. So, as a discounter, he would just never pay the going rate for anything in the business – it'd be a sin to do so!

Now the business has grown looking after international and national brands which remains to be the focus, but of course when a friend asks you to create a website for them, you can't turn them down!

Wolf Entertainment

The second business I set up was a production company set up for feature TV production, television formats and content distribution. I wanted to take creativity to another level – the idea came by during a trip when I would brainstorm ideas – so it's important to get that pen to paper to translate what's going on in your mind into black and white, simply because you can forget about it, then go back and read what you've noted and either say, 'What was I thinking?' or 'What a good idea that is.' During my time as the Monopoly man, I met a team of 'geniuses' in the TV industry. These guys had created the best-selling TV quiz globally, selling the format to over 100 countries and securing multi-million-pound revenue. I was heading a project and commissioned these guys to create a brand-new format, and as we got to know each other, I was amazed at their work and what it involved. We flew out to Belgrade where we held talks with a national frequency operator, and it was while we spent more time together that I began to learn about how some of the most iconic shows in the UK were made. These were shows that you grew up with in the eighties and nineties, the shows that you and your friends would run home to watch so you don't miss them. There was no catch-up TV back then!

I learnt so much from our time together that I knew one day, this is what I'd like to be involved with: TV production! The first step was to learn about what services I could offer in this sector, then the next step was what can I create that's original? So, I started writing and writing ideas about shows and series. I called around broadcasters that I'd worked with in the past, although they might not be the correct department to talk to, and I explained what it was I was doing in the hope that they would introduce me to the right person.

As a rule of any business trip, I always pack my day with as many meetings as possible, so an idea would be 45-minute meetings from 9am to 7pm. Yeah, that's 10 meetings where travel permits! From experience, if you travel just for that one meeting and it fails or nothing comes of it, you haven't used your time wisely, and as for a 'little break' – I'd rather sit at home and switch off!

To put that into perspective, on one of my trips I was faced with of a hard-nosed businessman who was the commercial director of a large television station. He was in his sixties, had a moustache that resembled Mr Potato Head's, and he didn't want to hear from some kid from the UK who was trying to sell him a TV format. His goal was to crap all over the idea, tell me he could do it all himself – then he'd go and brag to his colleagues and CEO how he made a guy fly from London to sit in front of him while he tells him who the real daddy is!

Why would he do this? Ego! That's one of the most important things in carrying out business: tiptoe around people's ego – if you're trying to do business with someone who needs to feel important (which you'll pick up in their mannerisms and tone of voice), and if that's something you can work with, then go with it. Don't tell them the opposite of their ideology as you're not there to be their counsellor – let them deal with that. Just keep it simple and deliverable.

Well, in my case, if you do go against their train of thought, it can turn out rather unpleasant. 'You've got to be kidding me! I'm offering you the opportunity to have a global show come from your TV station and you think you can do it without us? You're producing trash television and the world doesn't want to see that.'

After I realised what I'd said in the heat of the moment, I shut up and looked across the desk.

'Look, I know everything there is to know about television. I don't need Tom, Dick or Harry to tell me what to do. You think you brainy Brits know everything,' he said, and as he slowly tipped his cigar ash, I had the feeling his moustache would fall off. He seemed a little shook.

I realised I'd hit a nerve and there was no saving this one, so I left. Sometimes it's good to show emotion. It means you care about what you are doing and take pride in it. Sometimes, however, it can lose you a deal, just like this one. But, longer term, you need to be aware that people do business with people, so if there's a personality clash, you can bet your bottom dollar it's not going to get any better down the line, only worse.

Thankfully, the whole trip wasn't a car crash like that meeting. I had set up another meeting with another broadcaster who got the show, they got it! It made sense from every angle! Since then, we've created a documentary, are ready to produce a new six-part series, two feature films and a project that may involve Hollywood!

In Short Supply

Now, you'd be silly to leave a job where you've built a business and built a fantastic network of contacts and just put it all in the bin, right? I mean, there would be an ethical question as to if you are going into competition with the company you've just parted with, sure! But I found a little nugget, and that was selling clearance and overstock!

The first deal came about simply from an old client sending me an email saying that they had $500k of old stock they couldn't sell, and was there any way I could sell it for them. I took a look at the stock and got to work sending out offers and talking to people over the telephone, and within a short space of time – sold! Seven trucks sent out to collect the goods, buyer happy, seller happy, me – very happy! I had just realised there was an easy way to make money! Except, of course, nothing is easy, and I needed to find more of this stock to make a business out of it.

During the start of the coronavirus period, I learnt quickly that there was a need for various traditional stores to be able to trade their excess stock as a result of lockdown. I put together an operation that trades excess stock of FMCG, freeing up space and delivering liquidity to the client. I started to reach out to people from all over the world, some whom I had relationships with and others I didn't. One of the biggest wins was being able to shift stock from less developed countries who were not functioning online to those that were bursting with online sales.

There is a next stage of expansion to the business, but in these uncertain times, what matters is the bottom line!

Now, the best part of this business model is that you don't need anything apart from a telephone and email. You don't have to buy the stock, store it, pay for transport – absolutely zero. There are plenty of ways to skin a business model, right down to its bare bones, in order to make it profitable and sustainable. This model is based on brokering stock, but you are also responsible for the delivery of that stock from A to B and for ensuing that the stock is in the condition the seller states. There are various legal mechanisms you can create to ensure that everyone involved is protected.

But the bottom line here is, if you want to start a business, you can do it without putting in a penny of investment! The only investment is your time to make it happen!

CHAPTER

9

Only Fools and Boycie

Only Fools and Horses is Britain's most watched sitcom ever, and the best sitcom ever made if you ask me and millions of people in the UK. It's one of those shows that can resonate with almost anyone. Also, the characters in the show can easily be identified with in your own family and friends in everyday life. I guess that's just one of the reasons why the show has been so popular, alongside the phenomenal writer, the late John Sullivan.

It was October 2019 and my sister asked me to accompany her to go and see Boycie from Only Fools and Horses talk to an audience. Well, my sister rarely asks me to go anywhere with her, and it was no surprise that I wasn't first on her list. Her husband was working, our uncle didn't feel great and somewhere down the line was me. I know that she's a huge fan of the show so, of course, I did the good deed and cleared my schedule to go with her – because if I didn't go, she wouldn't go! As we walked into the venue, she said, 'There he is! It's Boycie,' and starts to shake.

So, I said to her, 'Go and talk to him.' 'What do I say?' she asked.

'Hi would be a good start,' I said.

With a slight push forward from my palm to her back she was standing in front of Mr John Challis AKA Boycie.

'Hi, hi Boycie.'

'Heellllooooo!' said John Challis in the famous Boycie tone. I felt for her. There she was, gazing at John Challis with puppy dog eyes and completely speechless. Of course, I could have been that brother who'd let her sink and afterwards beat herself up over it, but I couldn't do that. So, I entered the conversation and started talking, explaining that my sister is a huge fan, how popular the show is in Serbia etc. and to my surprise, Boycie had already visited Serbia! Can you believe that?

Carol, John's wife, was there, and she explained how lovely it was to see the show's popularity in that part of the world. All the while, my sister was starstruck and nodded away with an expression on her face that read: 'OMG! THIS IS HAPPENING, I'M STANDING, TALKING TO MY FAVOURITE ACTOR!'

As the show was about to start and just before John walked away, I said, 'Well, the next time I see you we'll be filming a documentary in Belgrade.'

Where that came from, I don't know, but it made sense to me!

Off we went to watch the show, and during John's talk he went into a little bit of detail about Belgrade and his visit a few years back. So, there I was in the stands, and the cogs were turning away in my head, and I've convinced myself I was completely right about our trip to Belgrade. Of course it should happen.

After the show we said goodbye, I left my details with John and Carol and we arranged to meet in the future.

Now, my sister was in complete shock all the way home, so I played the cool brother: 'Yeah, well, look, I only came this evening to make sure you could attend. If something comes of this, great. If not, I'm happy that you met him.'

Everything I said was true, but I played it out in such a 'cool' way that it could elevate my status from 'little brother' to, almost, a 'big brother'.

The next day I started brainstorming and I decided I should send an email with some of my ideas of what we should do next. My thoughts were: this was the best way for me to showcase what I am capable of and above all what an honour it would be for me to work with such a legend! So, I started brainstorming and typing away, then I hit send and waited patiently.

After a few hours, 'ping'– email reply received!

We agreed to meet in Kensington the following week to discuss what we could do and what was achievable.

The day came and off I went to the big meeting. I must admit it was like being with the most famous person on the planet. 'Excuse me, are you Boycie?' 'Can I get a picture with you?' Our meeting wasn't on a park bench either. We were at a 5-star hotel in Kensington, where of all places you would think that this sort of thing would be toned down. Well, I guess it all depends on who you are; the iconic John Challis is a national treasure!

After being interrupted several times during the meeting, we eventually got on with it and I discussed the plan of how we'd shoot this documentary and then we started looking at dates.

'We can do January, which is two months away, or we can do somewhere in June?' said his wife.

'January, let's do it,' I said.

'Are you sure that isn't too soon?' she said. 'Nope, I'll make it work,' I said.

As you'd have noticed I can be very impulsive, what I didn't want here was for a project to be dragged out and then end up taking a back seat because maybe John Challis got something a bit more attractive offered to him.

I thought to myself, it's a documentary, not a Hollywood film with millions behind it. Let's get out there and get it done!

In hindsight, how lucky do you think that was, filming a documentary in January 2020 before lockdown in a foreign country. If I had made the decision to do it in June 2020, I still wouldn't have even shot it by now.

The documentary was to be an exploration of why Only Fools and Horses is the most watched show in Serbia, which you have to admit is a pretty bizarre fact!

The next day I got on the phone and started planning, from locations to visit, to accommodation, flights, arranging my production team to be on site, the whole lot. This was going to be great; I had to make sure I was all over it!

We arrived at Belgrade and the first thing I heard was 'Boycie, is it you?' in a deep accent. A large gentleman walked over, smiling from ear to ear, said thank you to John for bringing him so much joy from the show, took a picture and moved on. Then the next person and the next person – at this point I just wanted to get to the hotel! Boycie was received as a national hero in Belgrade, with his hosts rolling out the red carpet almost every place he visits. He visited the British Embassy, the largest Orthodox Church in Europe which was under construction (the Temple of Saint Sava), Red Star Belgrade Football Club, a brandy distillery, a royal palace and a motor museum which had the yellow reliant regal there. There was nothing we didn't explore, and a media storm occurred everywhere we went. Everybody wanted to talk to 'Boycie'.

We spent just over a week in Belgrade for what would be one of the most memorable and joyful times in my life. The amount of laughter I had in the week with John Challis and his wife Carol was off the scale. It was full of fun and jokes; everything had a story to it.

One of the funniest moments was when we were pulling up to the motor museum and, while parking up, a police officer walked across the road with his machine gun across his chest:

'You can't park there, but can I get a picture?'

It was hilarious. John, who was half shook up, half ready to burst out laughing, wasn't sure what he should do!

Of course, during the trip I had technical meltdowns with the crew and a number of things that didn't go right, but why bore you with that? Everything we were recording was unscripted, I wanted to capture authentic reactions from John and from the public, so if we lost the shot, or someone wasn't quite ready for the shot, there was no 'from the top' retake – it was a case of 'It is what it is.' I think that's what kept me sane, I didn't dwell on, 'Well if we caught that shot it would have been great.' Nope, no time for that, let's move on!

Back in the UK, the following weekend, we visited John for some more filming and off the footage went to my guys in post-production. What a relief!

The time I spent with John and Carol was priceless, not only because I was fortunate enough to have been part of such a memorable project, but I also made some friends for life. We kept talking and sharing views on the documentary, then on one visit I had an idea that we should create a poker set. One of the most famous episodes of Only Fools and Horses is called 'A Losing Streak', where Boycie tries to cheat Del Boy out of a poker game by having four kings up his sleeve, only to learn that Del Boy was cheating too, only with four aces.

The idea was born to create 'Boycie's Four King Poker Set'. As the name suggests, it would be a poker set with an extra four kings to keep up your sleeve – what a great Christmas present that would be. All of a sudden, I found that part of me was so in touch with this iconic sitcom that it started to hook me in.

From my toy days I found a factory that could produce the set in China. I got my team to put the designs together, place an order and wait. A few months later, an email arrived back: 'Sorry, due to coronavirus we can only deliver in February 2021.' The units were on pre-sale and we'd sold hundreds already. What could I do? Cancel the orders and refund the money? What other options were there?

At this point, after a little panic, I decided that if I was going to make this product it would have to be made in Britain. It would be more expensive, but at least we were helping the British businesses in such a time of uncertainty. I found a supplier for the cards, then another for the box, one for the poker chips and the list went on. It turned out to be a lot more expensive in the end, but we still turned a profit and kept the customers happy by delivering a product, so it was a win-win situation!

The poker set arrived, and it was beautiful, luxury feel and crisp – I'm immensely proud of what we achieved. The orders were shipped out, customers were happy – everyone's a winner! During the summer of 2020, things became a bit more relaxed. Europe had loosened its restrictions and I noticed the cinemas were re-opening. Instantly, I thought, 'What are they going to show? Surely there is a hunger for production?' I got in touch with the largest cinema chain in Serbia and started pitching.

After some time, we had a deal for all the cinemas in Serbia and Montenegro to show this documentary. Could you imagine the delight I was feeling? Me? Having a film in a cinema? WOW!

Now, don't get me wrong, there were some hurdles for getting it into the cinema, as they rarely screen documentaries. Even though the pandemic had hit film production, you still had films that had a few million pounds budget not getting into the cinema too, so it wasn't an easy ride by any means.

I decided to get in touch with the local cinema chain in the UK for them to screen it too, which they were happy to, but unlike Serbia, the situation in the UK was more difficult as people were not as comfortable going to the cinema. Regardless, the film was shown locally too!

Alongside launching the documentary on Blu-ray, DVD and the poker set, a whole range of merchandise was created from mugs to art prints.

All of this happened because I took my instinctive decision to make it happen! There was no plan, no prior brainstorming; it all happened off the cuff. If this doesn't prove that you can make it happen, I don't know what can! It's all down to you!

We've now got more projects planned, but work aside, it's so nice to be able to make friends with people who are genuine, care and know how to make you laugh!

That's the real win here!

10

To be continued

It was a cold and wet October nearing the end of the disastrous year that was 2020. So much doom and gloom and now we were having the horrible weather to top it off. I received a phone call from a friend who I hadn't heard from in some time, and he explained that there was an opportunity to launch a radio station with a legendary presenter who was between two stations and looking to bridge. Curiously, I probed him for more details, and the more I dug into the story the more I learnt about the potential. I kindly told him to leave it with me and that I'd be in touch if there was something I could do.

So, this broadcaster is a big name in the music industry from the seventies and eighties, renowned in his speciality, so I got thinking and made a few calls. Before I knew it, I'd parked the radio opportunity and gone with TV. With all due respect, my initial thought was that most people listen to the radio while commuting, so with COVID and lockdown, surely engagement had gone down, and more people were glued to their screens? It turned out that I was right, and I found myself on a journey to creating a television station.

How did that happen? Well, my first train of thought was you need a team of people with experience, people who can deliver within the entertainment industry. Remember that nice chap that helped out with our Lifeline events? Yep, I gave him a call and explained the opportunity that was on the cards. His team deliver all day long within the entertainment industry and they had just set up a virtual studio delivering streams from their studio and connecting people all over the world adapting to the current events industry climate – they are clever guys! Well, he was interested, and they'd be happy to be our technology partner for this project.

The first board meeting was set up and the technology partners sat down with us and discussed their capabilities of what could be done with their equipment and studio space. It was all a little surreal, but I took charge and steered the direction of the meeting. I needed to share the vision I had so everybody could feed back with their own thoughts. My idea was that we could bring original content to the platform that would be entertaining and over time acquire content that we could play out.

Just like that, we started with our first show, which was a live feed of a breakfast radio show, followed by a morning/late night show which really was entertaining in many ways. But we tested the capabilities of the production and what we could deliver.

We weren't broadcasting to a national frequency or cable television; we were only streaming to our website, which was a saviour in terms of Ofcom fines, for sure. It was all a learning curve for us in many ways, but what quickly developed was that a team of 20+ people were enjoying what they were delivering (under pressure) as we were not rehearsing anything. We were hitting the ground running, learning how to work together and produce live television. The feedback we were getting from those tuning in and watching was fantastic too, so it ticked all the boxes in terms of what the platform was trying to achieve. However, the task ahead to make it into a channel was mammoth.

So, when you've got the feel of what it is you need to do and you've done a little bit of it, what next?

You grow!

Over Christmas we all had to take some time out. Within one month we had produced 18 live morning shows, six original talk shows and over 20 live streams of the breakfast show – over 40 hours of original content. To put that into perspective, an hour of television can cost anywhere from £20,000 to £100,000 per hour … so it was a heck of a lot!

Even when I switch off, my mind is subconsciously thinking of solutions and planning ways forward. Although I was taking time out, at the back of my mind I was still thinking about what to do next, but for sanity and health, after so much immersion, you need to get out of the water and breathe, take a look around, plan and then get back in!

At this moment in time, we're now working with popular shows that have been broadcasting from home during lockdown and working with them to bring their show to our studios and platform. We're also working on brand-new shows and also, importantly, securing the rights to a lot of content that we plan to broadcast on our platform.

While the plan is there and it may sound easy, there's an awful amount of work to do to make sure everything is right and in place. There are so many things that could go wrong and, of course, there are so many things that can go right.

One thing that is different to this commercial venture than to all the other ones I've spoken about is that I'm a founding partner; it's not something I 100% own, like I'm used to. It's a different approach as everybody has their share of work and piece of the pie. So, it'll be an interesting journey for me, and I'm intrigued to see how it all pans out. Maybe I'll be able to share more about it in my next book? Who knows?

The takeaway from this story is that what may initially be presented to you as an opportunity may not actually be the full potential of the opportunity. Look for the opportunity within that opportunity. If you feel the offer isn't for you, think about how you would like it to be. What value can you bring that will not only make the opportunity more attractive to you, but also give it a higher chance of being a commercial success?

Remember, it's all down to you to make it happen!

PART II:

THE MAKE
IT HAPPEN
MINDSET

The Make It Happen Mindset

You've read my stories on how I made various things happen, and you're probably thinking – what was going through his mind? What was he thinking?

During this part of the book, I'm going to attempt to explain how my mind works when dealing with opportunities to make things happen!

There's no structure set in stone or any specific order that I go through, but there are certain processes or levels that I follow which mainly come instinctively when tackling a new project.

Let's just be clear: I'm not selling you a 'make it happen' plan or lifestyle; I'm sharing the way I work, and I hope you can take something from it!

11

Mindset

There are so many motivational speakers, coaches and mentors out there, and each of them will have their own way of teaching you various skills. For the record, I don't knock them – if each person helps just one person become better, that deserves praise! If everybody could do it, the world would be a better place.

Now the brain is the most complex organ we have, so our mind is always racing at lightspeed. Getting that information from your brain and translating it into a language you can comprehend while making a note of it is pretty tough, especially when you're trying to capture all of the detail and record the ideas/plans you have.

There is a lot of research on 'mindset' that one can look up and study, but what I want to do is explain my take on mindset. Positive mindset, growth mindset and all the other types of mindsets that have been researched, studied and evaluated are of course credible, and there is so much to learn from those papers and theories.

But I'm about to be the guinea pig to explain the 'Make It Happen Mindset'.

Now, to profile a 'Make It Happen Mindset' – let's say you're standing in a queue at a supermarket checkout and there are people in that queue: one who's getting served, the next one in line, the one behind him and you. Yep! You! You're last in line. The one that's getting served is happy; he's getting his job done, bagging his groceries, paying for them and going home. The next one in line is eagerly waiting. He knows he's next, he just can't wait for the person to finish and hey, they'd better not start talking and wasting time, because I'm next! The third person in the queue is also waiting patiently. He knows his turn will come, but he's looking around casually, and if he spots an opening, it's likely that he'll move. Then, there's you, back of the queue, what a shitty place to be in! Everybody hates being at the back of a queue! Who knows how long it's going to take you to get served? I guess you just want to get out of the store with your purchase and get on with your day, right? What do you do? What are your options?

Wait?

Leave the store?

Go find another checkout to get served elsewhere? Create an opening?

OK, so you get the first two, maybe the third? But what

about the fourth? Huh?

It's pretty simple. The third option is to lose your last place and move around the store to the other checkouts, as maybe there's a shorter queue elsewhere. The risk is you don't find any and you come back and become potentially even further back in the queue. But you can take a calculated risk and it's not so risky, so you go for it. This is what I call a 'mover'.

Now, how do you create an opening at a supermarket so you can get served and go home? This is where you are in your own domain and completely create an opportunity. Do you go to customer services and explain that you've got a valid reason to be served and need to leave the store quickly?

Or perhaps you ask an assistant to open the next checkout to help them handle the flow of customers coming in?

Whatever it is you do that makes you go from number four to number one quicker than everyone else means that you would be traditionally called a 'shaker'. However, I'm going to call it a 'Make It Happen Mindset'.

Now, this example was completely hypothetical – I guess it depends on how good you really are to be served under such circumstances.

This example is a great way to explain real-life situations, so let's compare it with your job. You may be the person who's being served; what that means is you're content, you have a job, a life outside your job and you're loving life – winner! You may also be the second person in the queue. Now, that's you in your job, but you're waiting for that promotion, you know it's coming, just not quite sure when. It'd be silly to leave, because you're there, that's what you've worked towards and it'd be foolish to lose it. If you're the third person in the queue, then you are sailing along, things are OK, there's no big rush, you're generally happy, but, if you spot something better, you're going to bolt like a horse and get out of there. Now, if you are the fourth person in the queue, then you know you're in a bad place and you need to move. It's going to hurt to stay where you are, but you know you'll get the result in the end. What you don't want to do is to wait so long that it comes to the point where you're ready to leave the queue and the supermarket, as that's not going to be a good result – nobody wins! What you need to do is start hunting and find that opportunity, and, if you can't find it, then you need to create your own one. That is of course, if you don't mind going back to the queue to end up finding out that you're not number four anymore, but maybe number five or worse, number six.

This analogy of the supermarket queue and your career moves does determine your current mindset. Think about it – where are you in that queue? Now, regardless of where you are in that queue, how do you feel?

Person one who's getting served might be in a really bad place mentally and having a meltdown.

Person two may be dealing with a lot of stress at work and at home.

Person three might have just won a little bit of money on the lottery.

Person four might have all the time in the world and you know what, they love the supermarket!

What? Huh?

Exactly, circumstances change everything.

You shouldn't be focused on money, winning all the time or always being the best – you should be focused on fulfilment, doing something that you enjoy doing, something you have a passion for. I'm a believer that we are all on this planet for a reason. Whatever it is you are doing (within reason), you are doing it for a better place to live in.

However, sometimes the situation may not be so clear cut – for example, if you are washing windows on an office block like my father used to do when he came to the UK. He was cleaning those windows not only so that the office block would look clean, but also for the people who were in those offices stuck inside all day sitting at a typewriter or on the phone, so when they'd want that little escape, they could look out of that window to the outside world and reset for that second or two.

Now, if that clean window helped one person, then by the time he had cleaned a number of windows, he would have made a lot of people feel good. On the other hand, you could look at it with a negative mindset and say, 'Ah, he's wasting his life cleaning windows.' In fact, whether he'd end up as that being his only job for the rest of his life, or a job until he found something better, he was providing for a family. What needs to be clear is that there is no shame in the way you earn money, whether you are cleaning the streets or trading on a market – as long as you are earning legally, you are winning!

And for that alone you should be proud, because whatever you are doing is having a knock-on effect on the economy and those around you. If you're happy with what you're doing, you are the real winner!

If you're not happy, you need to start making changes to make yourself feel better. It may be work or it may be personal – it could even be a combination of the two. But whatever you do, you must keep it simple. Think about it, will it work? If you think so, then do it, but if you don't believe in it, then you've already lost in which case, don't do it – you'll only disappoint yourself if you're doubtful from the beginning.

I always filter everything down to the simplest form, and for me, it works all the time. Ask yourself the simplest questions that just require yes and no answers and you'll soon find yourself making an all-important decision much quicker than you usually would.

The main reason is that those simple questions lead to simple answers, which means that you arrive at the destination you need in order to make a decision. Once you are there, you need that tunnel vision, focus, determination, and that all-important plan of action to go forward. But whatever you do, don't overcomplicate the opportunity so much that you talk yourself out of it. I have so often spoken with people who would explain a new business they thought they were 'ready' to take on but then it turned out that there were things in the way. For example, they might say, 'I want to start it up, but I'm going to be moving to a new house soon, so I will wait until I've settled in.' In, fact, nothing happens, nothing materialises – all because they've talked themselves out of it and they don't want to make it happen as much as they make you think that they do.

Be that person who is doing things, not talking about them – we've all met a character like that in life. You know that person who's doing this, that and the other, but the bottom line is that they're not delivering any of it. The problem with talking a lot about a load of different things that never materialise is that you will never get stuff done because a) you talk too much b) you're not delivering any of it apart from hot air and c) nobody wants to work with someone who just talks.

Generally, I try to stay away from these sorts of people, because they tend to bring confusion, as within a small conversation you've had with them, it seems at the time that you've solved all the existing problems but, in fact, you haven't at all; you've only ended up listening to how they'd solve it. There's no action, just talk… and we all know, talk is cheap!

But I realise that you want to be somewhere which right now seems unachievable. That's good, you've accepted that you cannot be where what you want to be instantly. Now start planning in phases how you will achieve that dream job or business. Let's say the idea is that you want to have your own fashion line and your own stores on the high street. So, you start designing, start making, start selling and grow. Yes, there is nothing ground-breaking in what I'm saying here, but life is indeed that simple. If you want to do it, go and do it. Find a way, only your hunger to achieve can make you achieve it. Remember that supermarket queue, if a problem arises in your plan, you find a way around it – there is always a way to achieve your goal and only you can find it – no one else can do it for you; that's the 'Make It Happen Mindset!'

There never is a right time for anything; life is full of surprises. We all like the ideal scenarios but come on, be truthful, not everything is ideal. Especially when it's down to you to make the first move. It's getting out of your comfort zone so much that you never are comfortable anymore. Once you're in this mindset, you'll be making things happen in no time!

I hope that my mindset approach can help you make those things you want happen! If you ask me, there is no magic wand or secret easy way to achieve your goals. But the way to do it is to simplify absolutely everything you can so that it's clear, concise information that you can handle in the least possible amount of time needed.

If sometimes you're feeling a little flat, stuck or burnt out because you may have been overcomplicating things or getting distracted, then maybe a re-read of this part of the book will help you get that boost that you need to get up and go!

What are you waiting for? Go and do it!

12

Thought process

You've got an idea, but have you thought it through? How many times have you heard that – hundreds of times I bet. The process of thinking it through is so important, but I see this as the stage before planning. Thinking an idea through for me is the most enjoyable part. But an idea without any thought or action – is only an idea!

How often do you daydream? Or how often did you used to daydream? We've all done that, some more than others, but you know when you're in a situation and your mind slips away, into another world and off you go, daydreaming about something not relevant to the situation you're in at the moment. You find it as an escape, you're visualising something else and you find it comforting.

Whenever I think through a project, business or decision I tend to visualise it, experience it, daydream about it. Why?

Well, if you can't see yourself doing it, perhaps you're not entirely convinced that it's what you should do. You've got to experience what it's like to walk in those shoes and make that decision, start that business or close that deal. It's almost like practising, preparing yourself for the big day.

I've always had a vivid imagination as a child and I'm sure at some stages I must have been the 'cheapest kid' to look after in terms of toys. I say that because as a child in the nineties, the Argos catalogue was the bible for toys, pretty much as it is today, but back then the catalogues were huge, reams and reams of paper would go into making this catalogue and there wasn't anything you couldn't find. What I used to do was stare at the toys I was interested in – as a kid, sure you want to have all the toys, but I quickly figured out I couldn't get all the toys – pocket money was weekly and sometimes I'd have to wait weeks to get that one toy I wanted. By the time I came around to buying that toy I'd not only know the page number of the product, but the catalogue number off by heart – you know, that number that you'd write down to pay for the product at the till – 465/4587 qty 1 – yeah, that one!

Well, I remember this one toy, it was a microphone and not just any microphone, oh no! This microphone could transmit your voice to FM radio, I think it was something like 106.0 FM you'd tune into and you're on the radio, it was amazing! Well there was only one problem – it was never in stock. You'd visit Argos, queue up and hear, 'No, sorry, not in stock, try again next week'. There was no click and collect or even a way to reserve the thing! The more I couldn't get it, the more I wanted it. So I used to sit at home and stare at this toy for hours imagining I'd got this microphone and that I was a DJ. As sad as it sounds, it made me happy, it was the closest thing I could get to having that toy! When I did finally manage to get it, oh boy! I tested it, how far could I be away from the radio and it would pick me up. To my surprise it was almost to the other end of the street. So what did I do? I sent out letters to the neighbours to listen to my station at 6pm on 106.0 FM and I played music by holding the microphone to a portable cassette player. When the track finished, I'd talk and tell jokes. All of this was possible because of my imagination and then translating it to become reality.

So whenever thinking about a project, I tend to take a moment and let my mind run away with the possibilities. What could happen, where, how, why, when all of these scenarios would run through my head and I would visualise how I'm going to tackle it – should I then face that problem later in waking life, I would know subconsciously how to deal with it. After childhood, when I started to take sport seriously on a professional level, one of our coaches would swear by visualisation techniques, which is very common in sports. On rest days, you would take time out to think about how you move on court with the basketball, actually visualise yourself bouncing the ball, running, shooting a three pointer and so on. Although you were not physically working out, psychologically you were training and triggering muscle movements which was all great practice and it seemed to work for me. Give it a go!

Remember everything that you are thinking through to write down, write down those questions you are asking yourself and also the answers if you have them. The more you tend to think through projects, the closer you become to that subject, you gain more focus and pay more attention to what it is you are searching for. Let's remind ourselves, what you are also thinking through is how it will work, but what you also need to think through is, what if it doesn't work? What then? What's the next move? How do you overcome this?

There is the danger of thinking 'I'm going to do this' and avoiding all the serious pitfalls, because you are saying to yourself 'I'll make it work'. That's fine in saying so, but you don't want to lose time if you fall and then scramble to put broken pieces together. That's when it becomes a mess, and you lose control and focus of the situation. It's one thing being confident, but it's another thing doing the homework behind the confidence so that if you ever hit that issue you thought about, you have an answer to it.

The reason I make reference to this is because I've had some people who have come to me for advice maybe with a completely different picture of what advice is. Advice is being honest, first of all with yourself and then others. Now one person came to me with an idea, that's all it was, but they had convinced themselves that their idea was ground-breaking, nobody had thought of it and that they were going to make millions. What they wanted was advice on how they move forward from the idea and make it a reality. What they weren't prepared for, was the questions I was about to ask.

The idea this person had wasn't something you thought 'Wow, why didn't I think of that?' – but was more of 'I thought you could do that already'. What they thought they had done was spot a gap in the market because several providers were doing something similar.

Hypothetically, let's say a business is doing very well because they are selling a wide range of drinks. However, they're not selling one of the most popular drinks in the market. So, this person thought, I'm going to sell that drink in a similar fashion to the business that's doing really well.

'Why isn't that business selling that product?' 'I don't know,' they said.

'Don't you think with all of the revenue that they are generating, they could already sell that product if they wanted to? They've got the perfect operation to do so.'

'Maybe they haven't noticed the gap in the market,' they said. 'What is your next step?'

'I thought you could look into it and make it work?' they said. 'How are you going to make this happen?'

'Isn't that what you're going to do, you're going to tell me how I'll make this work?' they said.

'You need to research and come up with a business plan – an idea is worth nothing.'

'I didn't come and talk to you, so you piss on my parade,

why are you being so negative?' they said.

Believe it or not, I've had a lot of conversations like this over time from family friends who seek to ask for advice. But they clearly haven't thought the idea through. If you just have an idea, that's all it is – an idea. Maybe there are hundreds or thousands of people thinking the same thing, but nobody is making it happen. There might well be a pretty good explanation for that too, maybe after looking into it deeper they realise that it just won't work, maybe it doesn't make financial sense or there is no market like you initially thought there was. But until you think an idea through, you have absolutely nothing but an idea. What you need to do is think it through – nobody in their right mind is going to do all the work for you just because you have an idea and nothing else – it just doesn't work like that. You need to make it happen yourself!

How many times have you heard, I was going to do that, but then they stole my idea? It's got to be one of the weakest excuses around – why not say, 'Yeah, I was going to become a millionaire, but my mate stole my idea, and they became one instead.' What a load of rubbish!

Imagine that everybody gave up what they were doing because someone was doing something similar? Like the ice cream van – imagine he said, 'You know what, I'm going to jack this in, there's another ice cream van in town, what's the point of me selling ice cream when there is someone else selling ice cream too, they stole my idea, they're copying me,

I better go do something else.' It would be silly, right?

Think about all of the businesses that are doing the same thing. For example, how many supermarkets are therein the same area? How many fashion labels? TV stations? Socks? Literally, there's so much competition out there but there is also a market, so even if your mate or colleague does steal your idea and run with it, why don't you still run with your idea if you've given it some thought? Surely the fact that you have had the initiative to think about the idea gives you a huge advantage!

You're already a few steps ahead, so there shouldn't be any distraction. But beware that after all your hard work, doing all the research and putting together a good business plan, someone you've shared your plans with doesn't go and steal it. Well, if that happens, then you are screwed – and I do pity you. This is exactly what happened to Nikola Tesla... a genius inventor way ahead of his time, who died penniless, and people are still using his inventions today... look him up!

Now your vision could be different from someone who has stolen your idea or just so happens to be another player at around the same time as you in some other remote part of the world and starting what seems to be the same thing. These factors shouldn't detract you; as the saying goes, only the strong survive; well it's true.

You've got to demonstrate that you've given your idea a great deal of thought and you understand what, why, where and how to keep running with it. That vision you have of yourself and that journey may not be necessarily the same as the other person with the same idea.

The best example I can give you is social media – so many people tried to make it work before, but they all failed to make it pioneering like Facebook did. There were a load of them like hi5, Bebo and Myspace – remember Myspace? It came with a default friend, the creator 'Tom Anderson' who had the same 'idea' as Mark Zuckerberg and was everybody's friend, but Myspace didn't make it as big as Facebook did – the common denominator in all of this is both of them having the same idea but not the same vision.

That's why it's so important to take time out, think your idea through and visualise what it could become. Then you start planning!

13

Planning

Y ou're ready to make it happen, you've got your idea, you've thought it through, now what?

Now it's time to act like a general, take charge and get planning – you need a plan of action.

This is where things start taking shape. You've pondered, researched and now you need a blueprint that's going to give your venture some backbone and assurance – these plans will ensure you've got all angles covered and that your roadmap keeps you on course for what is about to be a fantastic journey.

Where do you start? What's the first step?

It's all got to start from somewhere, so get writing down things that you think you need to have in place in order to make it happen and how to make it happen. Pretty much everything you've thought through needs to translate into a plan. Now, writing all of the random things that you need on pieces of paper will eventually form into a plan of sorts, believe me, but you've got to get through that process of writing what you need in order to achieve it. You can worry about the presentation of the plan later, as you'll find you may repeat a lot of your notes, or not all of them will be necessary by the time you have finely sculptured that plan of yours! But the first thing to do is to start writing.

Always start the plan with what it is you want to be doing. For example, a flower shop. Right, you want to have a flower shop selling flowers. So think what you will need. Clearly you will start with flowers. But after that, will you need an outlet? Fixtures and fittings? You get where I'm going with this! Then work all the way backwards in the plan and price things up, find the cost-effective option, or the luxury option, but it's much easier planning from where you want to be going backwards than going forwards. Why? Consider your destination – how many times have you sat on a plane and not known where you're flying to? Exactly, none, or if you have, you probably don't want to remember it. You need to know where you're going in order to achieve it. So, in this case, planning a venture (from my experience) is much easier planning backwards.

Once you've gone backwards – go forwards! The same principle applies here, only in the opposite direction. Where is it you want to take this venture? What are the other opportunities that lie ahead and could spin off this venture and lead to further opportunities for you? You've got to map out all the things you can see happening. If it is a bit crazy, write it all down. Afterwards you can cut things down if you find you want to, but do make a note of everything you believe can work.

Planning can be tedious for some people, as you'll always be looking at the finer details here. Some people may love nit picking every single little thing, whereas others may be thinking bold and are a little rough around the edges. The answer is – whatever trait you have it will be fine. However, what you'll notice over time is that you won't be able to carry on doing it all yourself, but when starting out, you're going to have to, unless you've got a team of people that are on board and putting it all together with you. The exciting part of planning a new venture is that you are planning a destiny for an operation that's about to give birth. You may not be ready yourself, but you know you need to put things in place, and in time, you'll be ready.

You know where the flower shop is going to be, how you're going to get there and where it's going. Great. But how much is all of this going to cost? You've got to do the maths behind it all, factor in all the expenses possible – don't worry about the total cost being sky high to start with. Build absolutely everything possible you may need to have to get going as nothing is set in stone. Once you've laid out all of that upfront cost, then go back over it again and again, and throw out anything you may think is unnecessary, like that chocolate fountain – it does look cool, but you don't need it!

Costs are done, now let's look at the forecast. If you've managed to research well, you may even have some first-hand information of what others in the same industry are turning over. This will help you better plan your cash flow for your business and also give you a target if not an idea of what you should be taking. Now don't worry if revenues aren't coming in as fast as you would expect them to – everything takes time, but your plan needs to allow for that buffer. The venture cannot be cash strapped, as cash flow is the lifeline to any business, and you don't want to be worrying about how you will pay your overheads each month. You want to be focusing on how to grow and on how much profit you'll be earning each month, so make sure a realistic sales forecast is in place and that you can afford to run the operation for a trial period of time. A trial period can be anything from six months, one year or more, but generally between six to twelve months you'll be able to judge what's going on, how well it's doing and any changes that need to be made.

Do you need a team? Who do you choose? Where do you find them? Most people tend to work with people they know when starting out. It makes sense, you know who you're working with, you trust them, and they understand the journey you are on and generally would like to be part of it. What can be difficult is when you start off with a complex venture, requiring specialists whom you may not know where to find. This step may be difficult, but in the end it can also be a lot easier having a professional relationship with them. If you enlist the help of friends and family who know you personally, various complexities can come out of that, whereas a strictly professional relationship has its boundaries and no history – working from a clean slate can sometimes be the best way to do it!

How will people know about you? The way to go is marketing! This is an important cost that you need to factor into your expenses.

If, on the other hand, the venture you have set up has already secured long-term work, then you won't need to market. Great – that means you don't need to focus on winning business, but just on delivery! However, even if you have got that contract, you should set aside something for entertaining those clients, although at the time of writing that has been hard to do due to the pandemic. But, pandemic aside, getting to know your client over food or a day out at a sporting event can not only be enjoyable but it's creating a friendship too, and you're showing your gratitude for them choosing to work with you as opposed to anybody else.

On the other hand, like most businesses, you'll still need marketing in some way or form. First of all, profile your customer. Who are they? What do they like? Where are they located? Really go into detail of who that person is that will be using your service. Once you're armed with that information you can start targeting that specific audience by using a range of tools from TV, online, print, radio and out-of-home advertising. In each of these channels there are layers and layers that you'll need to go through to pinpoint that exact profile, and the more specific you can be in targeting your customer, the better chance of success you will have.

Now depending on the type of venture you are setting up will determine whether you'll need some form of start-up capital or not. For example, if you are planning to leave your job as a graphic designer and start freelancing, the set-up costs are pretty much 0 as you are offering a service that you're already known for and there are so many platforms online that cost nothing to register and pitch for work. On the other hand, you may have designed a product that's now ready to be produced and to go into a large retailer that's going to pin you down on terms. This case is very common with new products going to market. If you've won a contract to supply say 200 stores, you need to pay for that stock to be manufactured, shipped and delivered to the client in return for waiting 30 – 90 days to get paid. Yep, it can be that painful on cashflow, but you've secured a sale, so what you need to ensure is that you've got the capital to see it through. If you haven't then there are various ways you can raise funding, but you've also got to factor in the cost of any money you're borrowing or a stake in the business for that capital. If you're going down this route, then don't just write down the amount you need. Account for any interest that's payable too, as if your bottom line of profit starts to look slim and you haven't accounted for any interest, it could wipe it all out and you end up with nothing, or even in debt – which isn't a good start to any venture!

Now you've got your bases covered and you need to plan your attack! How are you going to get out there and tell the world you're open for business? What's your message?

Are you the: Cheapest?

Most expensive? Best quality?

Only one supplying this service? Most trusted?

What are you? You first statement getting out there should be big and bold. Well, maybe not too over the top, you might not want to give out the wrong impression by sticking your fingers up to everyone and then sit there scratching your head asking why they aren't using you – but hey, who am I to judge; I think after 2020, any form of communication can win. From pissing people off directly to being so quiet nobody knows you're there ... it's going to be a learning curve for whatever you're doing in an ever-changing market, that's for sure!

The message has to be clear, and not overly complex. You need to be able to communicate exactly what it is you are offering easily and concisely. If you over-complicate the message it can just get lost, and that happens a lot! Now don't be primitive by any means (Flowers = over here!) but think of something that stands out (Your personal florist at your fingertips). Personalising your service is so important today, as with so many generic products and services out there we all want something that's a bit more personal. So whatever you can personalise without losing focus or adding a large cost to, do it. You'll stand out from the others and you'll be remembered for that product/service because you went that little bit further than others would – that little bit of extra effort might mean a lot for someone!

So, by now your plan of action is ready to go, timelines are in place, you know when your venture will be open and ready, you have planned budgets, forecasts, and a full business plan that you can always reference back to whenever you may need to check that things are keeping on track. Don't get freaked out if things aren't going exactly to plan – that's part of the journey that'll keep you on your toes, and hey, what actually – ever – goes exactly to plan? The main thing is, you've got a plan, you're not just 'winging' it all the way – that would only end in disappointment for you and you don't want that at all!

Now probably the most exciting part is left for you to do... and that's get out there and do it!

CHAPTER

14

Obsession

Now it's time to get down to business; your plan is done and you're taking action. One thing that will make you stand out from others is the amount of passion you have for what it is that you're doing. I mean real passion, not the salesman trying to sell you something by convincing you it's the best and as they talk to you, you think you hear some sort of script, yep, that's because they are saying the same thing day in and day out. Real passion cannot be mimicked – there is a certain way that it comes across which I can't really explain, but you can sense some sort of energy in the air, let's say, an aura. When someone is passionate about what they're doing, there are no two ways about it, you get it! It's those people you want to be working with and the main reason for that is regardless of their cost or the time taken, you know that they'll put everything into making that job great because they love what they do. You want them to be able to answer your call outside of hours if necessary, at 10pm or 6am in the morning because they take pride in delivering a great outcome and will do what needs to be done to deliver a great result.

It's that obsession with the venture you are about to start that needs to be in place. You want to know every single little detail there is so you can fine-tune things quickly or make drastic changes if need be, but you need to eat, sleep and breathe exactly what you're getting into. Obsession is waking up and getting on with the tasks ahead – it's not waking up, snoozing, taking everything easy and doing things when you feel like it. Obsession is when you are so into what you are doing that nothing can distract you from it. Your new venture is all you think about, you've got that tunnel vision – all that should be on your mind is how to make whatever it is you're doing a success. That is so critical because at a start-up stage, it's so easy to fall through the gaps because you've taken your eye off the ball.

Well, with obsession, you've got both eyes on the ball, all the time!

Have you ever seen an unfocused boxer going into the ring? Or a tennis player that goes on court and spends more time looking around than playing tennis? These elite sportsmen have the same thing in common, they are obsessed with their sport. Think about it – day in and day out, you're punching a bag, six to eight hours a day, every day, for years and years on end, or the tennis player hitting that tennis ball, serving; they're both repeating the same processes for years and years on end, fine-tuning every single bit of detail. These characters have the obsession with the sport, otherwise, they wouldn't do it. Can you imagine that for 15 to 20 years you are doing the same thing. That's pretty tough right? They love what they do, but there is also a balance to be in place.

If you become over-obsessed, then it has the complete opposite effect, you start to hate what you're doing. Once you end up going into a love-hate relationship, it's a rocky road and one from which not many come out of the positive end. So while being obsessed, keep it within reason; don't go too hard on it, just make sure that you know as much as possible about what it is you're doing and most of all, enjoy it.

At this stage, I need to make a point that I'm sure a lot of people may not like, but I need to say this now, and clarify later after I share the business side first. Whatever sector you are in, don't take much notice of what others are doing around you. I know a lot of people in various industries who have done this and instead of keeping on track with what they want to do, they start following a 'fad' or a 'trend' that can have some devastating consequences. This is simply because they're looking at what other people are doing and if those people have a good presence it may seem at the outset that they are doing really well, so it is tempting to move in. However, this means you are apt to be caught up in social media, which can be a really bad place to be checking up on your competitors. In fact, you should be taking as little notice as possible as otherwise you are taking the risk of watching your competitor instead of growing while somebody else could take the core opportunity away from you because you've taken your eye is off the ball.

The best example I can give you of this is Nokia. Nokia was the best mobile phone out there in the 1990s – no question about it. Then Apple introduced the iPhone. By the end of that same year half of all the mobile phones in the world were Nokia's – WIN! Now, there are many interpretations of this story, but the way I see what happened next was that Nokia were concentrating too much on what Apple were doing, they spent so much time on Apple that they launched the N97, the 'iPhone killer' model, which failed badly and with all that time and effort focusing on what Apple were doing because it was revolutionary and cool, they lost focus and they were gone!

Now imagine if they had continued to keep developing and taken little notice of what Apple were doing, there would have been a bigger chance they'd still be around today. But what Nokia did was to drop everything and look at Apple. This then meant they were bought by Windows' new operating system, they scrapped all of their in-house development software and all of a sudden, they were a nobody. This is an example of what can happen and what you need to be aware of when looking at competitors. Of course, you can't always play it safe and expect to achieve huge things – risks need to be taken. But remember to be obsessed with what you're doing and not what the other guys out there are doing.

This can also be related on a personal level; social media can fuel so much negativity and depression by simply people posting pictures. You know the saying one picture equals 1,000 words? That's the case here – it's all completely open to interpretation. Someone on the outset could look like they're doing great, but for all you know they could be having a meltdown.

I know many people on social media who are successful, but a certain few post content, which is loud and materialistic, as if they have something to prove. Now they tell me it's inspirational and their followers like it. But to me, it's all superficial, it's all a show – there are not a lot of smiles behind the camera believe me, and life is as tough for them as it is for most. But to an extent, they are obsessed with what they do and, in many ways... they'd be silly to throw it all away and go for something else.

What I want to tell you is that you need to focus on being you and not somebody else.

Everyone who respects you will always respect you, whether you are posting pictures on a yacht or on a bus. There's a lot more to life than material things, so don't think 'Why haven't I got that?' 'Why can't I do that?' – think 'good for them' or if you can't stand them, remove them – the same principle applies in business.

Be the best version of you, be obsessed with your own development and many achievements will follow!

As a child I loved to play video games: Dizzy, Double

Dragon, Doom, Mortal Kombat, Time Crisis, Crash Bandicoot right up to GTA 3 – that's where I stopped. I had hit 16 and I just wasn't as interested as I was before. But during my whole childhood I was obsessed with playing these video games. I remember my late mother begging me to go outside and play on such beautiful days! But I wasn't having any of it – whatever I was playing 'HAD' to be completed. I would turn the computer on early morning and by night-time I'd be turning it off to go to bed. I also remember the days when there wasn't an option to save your progress; that meant the computer stayed on 24/7 because you just couldn't lose all that hard work you put in to achieve where you'd got to. So, when I hear the term, 'Pull the plug' it does hit home and can rattle a nerve! Until I completed whatever new game I was into, I was completely obsessed with finishing it. I don't think there was a game that I never completed, one way or another. I say that because you'd always find a way to 'make it happen!' In some cases, that meant finding out what the cheat commands were, but after the first time I tried that, it would only spoil the whole experience and you wouldn't have that same enjoyment as before.

The obsession to progress from level 1 to level 100 wasn't negotiable – it had to be done. This is the same obsession you should have with whatever it is you are trying to achieve: you have to keep going, and if you trip up and start again, it's not the end of the world. Back at square #1 doesn't mean failure, it means you know what not to do next time, but you don't just give up. You battle your way through again in order to achieve progress. We all progress in life in many aspects. All ventures are the same – they start from nothing but can progress into something very special.

When you're obsessed with learning to play a new instrument or learning a new skill like juggling, you repeatedly do it until you are happy with your achievement. What's important here is that this obsession relates to your plan, as you don't want to only learn how to get to the first stage of your plan, you want to keep that obsession until you achieve the end result. That end result may be to set up the venture, grow it and exit (sale) or it may be to just to set it up and let the experts run it. There are so many possibilities, but that obsession with achievement will keep you on track to deliver what is needed in order to gain that end result.

Now I just want to clarify my view on obsession: it's OK to be obsessed with your venture. What isn't OK is that you become over-obsessed with anything that could lead to harm. Something that could harm yourself and others around you is not OK.

What you don't want to do is end up becoming delusional; remember it's OK for things not to go to plan. It's not the end of the world – so many ventures just don't work, they don't get off the ground. Most successful business leaders have experienced this, so you won't be alone, but you'll learn from it. It's important to keep as sane as you can throughout the process and not go too crazy over it.

Remember it's OK to put all your energy into your venture, but you've got to schedule time for yourself. Rest is what everybody needs, and forget those routine stories of:

5am wake up 10km run

$1m deal before breakfast

Make my way to the office to start my day.

Keep as far away from those kinds of stories as possible – make a routine for yourself that involves rest. You know your body better than anyone, so only you can schedule when/how you rest. Otherwise, you're going to burn out pretty quickly, so make time for exercise where possible, and make sure you have a healthy diet, but don't go overboard with trying to give everything in your day the best you can or you'll burn out instantly. If you're running, enjoy the time away from the screen/phone or whatever it is you were doing, but make it leisurely, enjoy nature and the fresh air, so when you get back to work, you don't have to call it a day because you've just finished the fastest 10k ever because in that case, you'll be too tired!

But as you would have understood from the context of this book, it's about digging in deep, rolling up your sleeves and getting to work. If your focus is there, you will achieve great things!

15

Ownership

There's one major thing when conducting business that you need to do it and that's 'own it'. Take charge, stamp your authority all over it, because in whatever way the tide may change, you have to keep at the front of the storm. It's all you, your idea, your plan, your venture – there's nobody you should be running to for cover.

Ownership is the backbone of you taking responsibility for everything you do. There are a lot of weak players out there who will seem to take ownership, but when something goes wrong, they are quick to pass the buck to someone down the line. If something messes up, take responsibility for it. Regardless of whether it was out of your control, if you had to perform a task and it didn't get done – then take ownership of that. The worst thing you can do is find a route to blame. Why? Well, that's because things can start to crumble, whether that's within your team or organisation. If a person doesn't want to take the responsibility of not delivering and would rather pass the ownership onto someone else within their team then that's only going to end badly. How many times have you watched The Apprentice, and then it comes down to two candidates that are about to get fired because a task didn't go to plan? I guess it's great TV to watch as it's all about entertainment, but when the bickering starts that's when I cringe, as it's either from one side or both. It's rare seeing someone say 'Yeah, you know what, that was my fault, I take full responsibility,' but, in fact, that is the type of team member you want on board. They are educated enough to take responsibility for their actions and are not afraid to admit faults – this is how you progress, learn and win!

A blanket approach can be used in various situations. If your role is to close a deal and you didn't close the deal because the person on the other end left their job when you were just one day away from signing, well, that's tough luck, but it's your ownership that will see it through so that a deal is done or that you find an alternative. Whatever the outcome you've got to remember you are the one that's heading the task and you need to find a way of making it happen!

The worst thing you could possibly say to a client who's upset about bad service is that you've got bad staff, or that an employee was bad and no longer with us. Personally, I'd prefer to hear integrity, for you to say, 'I apologise, that work just wasn't up to our standards that we usually deliver, and we hope to rectify this as soon as possible.' So much more professional, yet you are not putting anybody down, because you are already on the backfoot with the client not being happy. Do you think they really want to know about what goes on in your organisation? No, they just want the service they're paying for. In any case, you would only be demonstrating how bad your ship is and why it isn't sailing the way it should be. Do you think that will give the client more confidence? Or they'll pity you? As soon as they sniff a sign of something not being quite right, they'll go! This is a situation you'll never want to be in, but if you do end up in it, which most businesses do at some point, be honest, but remember to be a team player too, and don't sacrifice a team member to try to save some face – it doesn't work. Equally, if it's you that's made a bad decision, admit it, yep, that was me. I learnt from it and will improve, that's what it's all about. Now let's say you're providing a service for that client who's upset. Let's say you've made the client a diamond necklace that's worth a fortune, but the jeweller has added a small stone of a slightly different colour to the one specified. Now you've communicated with the client that it'll be corrected, the next stage is tackling that within your team. There's a distinct difference between ownership and blame. Blame will never get you anywhere, unless you are in the business of discipline, but what you need to do in a skilful manner is find out at what point did it go wrong, where and how was the error made? Once you've got to that point, it may be something as simple as a communication error or a bad judgement. The main thing is all mistakes can be rectified internally. If the errors keep on coming once you've addressed them, that's going to be when you'll need to take further action.

If you think you're going to be entering into a new venture without making errors, you are wrong. There are businesses out there that are hundreds of years old and they still make errors today. And don't forget that sometimes that error can lead to a new opportunity.

When you take charge you've got control, you're not waiting for anyone to give you the green light on decisions, that's all down to you. An example is the story earlier about me putting together the Lifeline 25th anniversary at Claridge's for the royal family of Serbia. It was something which I took ownership for, so if anything happened at that event it would be my ultimate responsibility. Regardless of whether it was a third party who was performing at the event or even a guest, when you own something, you're putting your name on it, and you will do as much as possible to make it great, because that's what you do. You don't want anything half-baked or for it to be remembered as an awful experience which you were responsible for, because the next time you go to do something similar, you've got to make it out of this world to make up for the last time!

There's an element of ownership that you don't want to fall into. It's that ultimate ownership of almost everything where you become the control freak. The funny thing about this is that it's such an easy trap to fall into – once you're inside, it takes a lot of effort to get out. Imagine filling a huge ball pit that's five metres deep – great, you own it, it's yours, but as soon as you jump in it, it's going to take a huge amount of effort to get out.

We're all guilty of this to some extent. You'll take on a few more extra tasks that maybe you shouldn't do because a) someone is getting paid to do it or b) you feel that you'll do a better job of it – but for whatever reason, you find yourself doing something you shouldn't be! Can you imagine a CEO of a luxury property portfolio packing up an exhibition stand by himself and loading up the truck – that would be mad, wouldn't it? Well, it's happened!

What's more, this CEO who has hundreds of staff in this sector sometimes sells the property himself to clients that have shown an interest in the developments that are being constructed. I just happened to be with such a person during a meeting, when they said, 'Hold on, I've got some buyers coming for an apartment, I told them I'd see them.' So off we went to see this couple at the reception sales desk where there is a team running around them serving refreshments. They greet each other and have a tour on site, talk through the plans, and see the apartment in the block which is for sale. All throughout the visit, this person is saying how they chose this location to build, they chose the architectural design of the complex, how they plan further development. And while these comments are being made, I notice the couple looking puzzled. They must have been thinking this cannot be the owner, surely – or perhaps they thought this sales agent is mad! I never found out what they thought, and they bought nothing in the end. But straight after the visit we sat back down and I said, 'Why are you doing this?

You have a team that deal with sales?'

'It's not the same experience, everyone likes to talk with the owner,' they said.

I politely explained that warning signals must have been running through their heads and that I doubt they'll buy anything now. This is where taking ownership to control freaks sends out the completely wrong signal and as soon as you present something that a potential customer wouldn't usually face, alarm bells ring, because the process doesn't usually flow like that. When was the last time you went to watch a film featuring, for example, Leonardo DiCaprio, and he was the one behind the counter selling you the ticket, giving you popcorn and showing you to your seat? Firstly, I'd guess you'd say it's pretty cool because you're a big fan, but it's not the service you'd expect and you'd think something isn't right here, am I getting pranked? These are the warning signals we all receive when we notice that something doesn't sit quite right. Instinct also tends to tell you to get outta there!

Ownership is fine but let others breathe. How many times have you seen quotes online along the lines of 'employ people who are more skilful than you?' Agree. Couldn't agree more. There is also something like 'employ attitude over skill, skill can be taught' – this makes me laugh. So, you employ someone who's got a fantastic attitude – I mean great, eager to learn, bright, smart etc. but you're about to send a rocket to space and they have no skill. It doesn't work – you need a skilful team, but equally your business culture should have that underpinning feel that breeds a good attitude. You should let others vent and tell you what their thoughts are without reserve.

There are so many cultures out there within businesses that when you walk into an office you can sometimes feel a tension so bad that you could slice it like a cake. These tend to stem from the top down, because whoever is in control is sending out the wrong vibes, which feed throughout the company.

If you can create an open-minded environment that allows for creativity and some fun, you'll benefit from coming up with solutions that perhaps the other competitors just wouldn't think of. That's because you are not dictating what should be done, but instead as you feed that culture down the hierarchy, those at the bottom closest to the end service/client feed back up and it becomes circular. If you can achieve this within your organisation you are at the pinnacle of business culture. That's because the bottom are feeding from you, but also the client/end user because they are content with the service, which feeds back up, giving you a boost in ensuring that the decisions that you are making are good ones.

What's important is that when taking ownership, you can adapt and change the way the market moves. 2020 was such a tough year for many businesses, but those that took charge right at the start in affected sectors were the ones that ended up winning! You may not have to be a pioneer, but you will have to be agile enough to make those all-important, critical decisions before time runs out. Ownership is taking absolutely everything into your own hands as a leader and making sometimes the toughest and most brutal decisions not only for survival but also for growth. With every element of a top-level decision there is risk, but risk is also something you own!

Remember your new venture is your baby; you've got to own it and take charge in order to grow!

CHAPTER
16

Delivery

Everything you've been talking about doing, thinking about doing, planning to do, obsessing about and owning all comes down to one thing – delivery! This is another important pillar within your business that should never be compromised. If this happens, you start to crumble. You know that saying 'they're only as good as their last job'. I never used to agree, but in today's environment if you're having a bad day or a bad time, there's not that loyalty that maybe used to be there in the nineties and before. People are quick to change their providers and move their business elsewhere. If your service doesn't deliver well and they find a cheaper alternative, they're gone. So now more than ever it's more important to make sure you deliver what you agreed to.

In business and in life, surround yourself with those who deliver. If you're having a bad time, but you know someone who's going to cheer you up then give them a call, because you know they'll be able to lift your spirits. You'll have a giggle and forget about whatever is going on, at least for a while. But you call that person because they'll deliver that entertainment, each and every time without fail. Don't surround yourself with those who talk about loads of things and don't deliver anything – why would you want to be surrounded by that? What stimulates the mind is making things happen, not listening to ideas of things happening. Have you ever called up a takeaway, made an order for delivery and it doesn't get delivered? No. That's how you need to process some of your actions; whatever it is, make sure you deliver.

Before you go promising that you can deliver anything, make you sure you actually can. There can be nothing worse than taking on a project of your own or one from a client that on the outset you think you can deliver and then find as you become more involved in the project that you cannot actually deliver. It's disappointing for yourself, but it's equally not fair on the client. Now I've been talking about making things happen all the way through this book! But everything has to be within your capabilities; this may be your first time undertaking such a venture, but there is an element of calculated risk. It is a bit like the non-skilled worker ready to launch a rocket in space that I mentioned earlier. If you're promising delivery of something that's way outside your reach, then you're taking the piss and you're being dishonest and basically a fraudster. You can't do shit like that.

How many times have you bought something, and it doesn't show up? Or you lend somebody money and you never hear from them again? These are feelings of frustration you get when somebody doesn't deliver. It reminds me of when I was opening my first toy store, and part of the store had a 'make your own teddy bear' section where there was a big machine that would be filled with fluff for the teddy bears. Well, a company in China could make them as well as more accessories to go with it, so I ordered a stuffing machine and an area which was like a bath, which blew air into the teddies. This would all arrive for the grand opening. It looked cool and it'd be made exactly how I wanted it designed. Many months went into making it look good and money was sent across, but then they said they couldn't deliver. The opening month of the store was October/November, and they could deliver only after Christmas – you could say I haven't had much luck with ordering from China, but I'm only highlighting the bad side, I guess. Anyway, this time I lost out on time and money; I never got my money back, nor did I take the goods, but it really worked me up!

Now let's talk about deliverables – these are the subtasks you're going to need in place to make sure the whole project/venture is delivered. It should always be going through your mind when taking on any size task or project. The main thing here is that you need to be brutally honest with yourself about the capabilities you have and any external research. If you think the project or venture is a 'stretch', which means it's within reach, you can probably achieve it. However, if it's something you're not comfortable with, but yet still think you can do it, then go and fetch a wider team to see if together you can make it work and then go back to the client with an answer. But if it's just not within reach and as much as you'd love to do it, you can't for a number or reasons, then you should turn it down gracefully. It may not sound like it, but in fact, I've turned down hundreds of projects. Nevertheless, for some of the projects I've turned down the clients have come back to me and asked if I could look after a particular part in that project, as opposed to the whole thing. So turning something down because it's not your bag, or because you wouldn't feel comfortable with delivery isn't a bad thing at all and doesn't necessarily mean you won't get any part of the project. This shows that it's best to go back and be honest!

How is your time keeping? Do you keep to deadlines? Regarding time keeping – on a personal level, I'm casual, and always have been. I'm the guy who promises to arrive at 2pm and turns up any time between 2:30pm and 3pm (only with my closest friends of course, that's the privilege). The reason for that is because I can never get away from what I'm doing – all of them know this rule by now, so now I'm the one that's always sitting waiting for them to arrive – it's only fair!

But in business, I'm always on time for meetings and if I'm running late, the client will know way in advance so they can make any adjustment that they need to, and so they're not waiting around for me wasting their time. The reason is that you need to respect everybody's time in the workplace. Get there as early as you can, perhaps 15 to 20 minutes early – that's great. Nobody likes sitting in a boardroom waiting for you and for the meeting to start and lose time, which will then have a knock-on effect on the next meetings for the rest of the day for everybody involved. Tardiness! Don't do it! You'll look bad!

How do you know if somebody can deliver?

If they haven't got a portfolio that you can check out and you don't know them personally, but you like what you are hearing, there will be that element of risk that you'll have to factor in. Remember the old cliché of 'if it's too good to be true, then it probably is'. However, in such a fast-paced environment sometimes you just haven't got the time to check them out. If they've come to you from a trusted source and it's something you're interested in and you're willing to take a small gamble on it that wouldn't hurt you too much if it didn't go to plan in the long run, then, by all means, go for it.

Really early on, I lost out to some stuff which I just couldn't get my head round. Because they were so simple, I thought, 'Why would people want that?' Guess what, they did, and now you've got operations like Deliveroo and Just-Eat. The one that landed on my desk and I had a meeting with was called 'Joey' as in the kangaroo – it was the exact same concept, but I just didn't see the benefit or appeal in it at the time. It was a pity as it was years ahead of the competition, but the market wasn't ready for it.

Timing to deliver is essential. If you peak too soon, you could be out. You hear about the stories that are along the lines of 'if I did it just one year earlier' – however, there are also stories where the project should have been done it a little bit later. Do you remember Ask Jeeves? The pointer nose butler with a funny quip? The idea was there; it was right, but the market just wasn't ready. The technique the search engine used was 'semantic search' (natural language queries) whereas ranking by hyperlinks is what's used by Google today – the problem was it was just way too early! Do keep this in mind when launching your venture – consider: is the market ready for this?

The best thing about delivery is that's when you can bill and get paid. If your deliverables are clear and you've completed them, you bill and get paid. There's nothing worse than agreeing for something to be delivered, but then the client wants to change x, y, z, which is stopping you from delivering, because the product isn't ready. This is the other end of delivery, where you are delivering, but the client wants last-minute changes.

This can be common in design, when providing branding for a client. Say for example they'd like a new logo. In that case, you'd work with the client to compile a brief, which includes what colour schemes they like, styles of font, and similar logos that catch their eye. And already with that information you have narrowed down your direction for the design to fit within what they are aiming for. The worst position you could be in is when you're taking on a project, but the client doesn't know what they want, gives you free rein, but then doesn't like what you have produced. In this case, you'll be on a road to nowhere and you'll find it hard to deliver the project. If the client doesn't know what they want to do and nor do they like the suggestions that you have put forward, then my advice would be that the client should come back to you when they know what they want. Or you'll be wasting your time on something that could be painful.

Otherwise, you should plan stage payments where the client will pay per design/concept or blocks of hours that will overcome the payment situation, so that rather than paying for the delivery of the finished project, they are paying for the deliverables. We've hired a lot of graphic designers over time who have been promised large projects, taking them on without charging and being left without payment or even delivery of the project to the client – because the client decides to pull the project.

What is the best thing about delivery? You get paid! So, whether you turn the project in deliverables with payment blocks or however you've safeguarded delivery, you've always got to be pushing for your venture to deliver so that it can bill and provide that much-needed cash to your venture.

If you can keep that cycle going consistently, you'll be growing cash flow in no time, and you'll be in a good place financially as well as building out a solid reputation.

You want to be known as the individual/business/

non-profit (venture) that can deliver. That's what's going to make you shine out among the rest as there are a lot of businesses out there, all of them delivering what they set out to do. But it may be that your specific skills or that service you are offering isn't fully available anywhere else, or that there is so much demand that the other businesses can't keep up. Well, whatever it is, just make sure that you are the one delivering in time.

I'd compare it to ordering a food takeaway: everybody likes the delivery guy when he's on time, and when he's not, you're probably not greeting him with a smile and a tip like you usually do, even though it's probably not his fault. But your food is cold, you're nearly halfway through the movie and the evening has not gone to plan.

This translates in exactly the same way in business ... so keep delivering ... on time! Again, all of this is simply me, the way I think and for you to take out of this what you think will be relevant to you.

PART III:

YOU

You

This final part of the book will be talking about the most important thing: YOU.

I'm going to attempt to challenge the thoughts that may be going on in your head in the search for anything that may be preventing you from going forward in life.

These will be questions that only you can answer yourself, but I hope that it will a way forward for you in that journey to making things happen!

The most important part of this is self-reflection. If you can relate to any parts that I talk about and it triggers you to think differently or tackle a certain trait or thought process, then I hope it'll help you go in the right direction.

CHAPTER
17

You do you

You've learnt about my experiences and the processes I use to make things happen, so what's stopping you from going out and making it happen!?

You?!

Self-doubt is the biggest winner in killing your idea, opportunity or passion. It'll eat away at it, until you give in and raise the white flag to self-doubt surrendering, before going on in exactly the same way you were before. Then there you are again, unhappy, not fulfilled, in the same situation, looking for another way out, another way to make things happen!

What's keeping you going is that there's something inside you that's telling you that you can do this. But where is it coming from? Most likely your heart. Sayings like 'heart of lion' aren't just a coincidence – yes you need to be smart and use your mind, but you need to make a clear boundary with where your heart can take you that your mind can't.

I was once told a story from a wise old man, who explained I was a winner from birth. In a nutshell, the story went along the lines of, from the millions of sperm that could have one, you were the winner; you were faster, stronger and more determined to make it than all the others in the race. What's stopping you now? He couldn't have made me laugh any more than he did when explaining it, but I sat back and thought, you know what, you're right! So, if life ever gets you down and you start to think you're a bit of a loser, how can you be? You've already won a race with millions of others involved. Once you start thinking like the winner you are, you're only going to achieve much more!

If you're doubting yourself then you need to dig deep and be honest with yourself about what's holding you back.

Fear of failure? Worrying that the venture won't work. Fear of humility? What will others think if you fail?

Fear of the unknown? Going from a stable income into something with no track record?

There are probably a hundred things going on in your mind, some positive, some negative, some completely contradictory, but through all of those mixed messages, you're going to need to find various ways to stimulate your thinking process to channel and clarify your thoughts. Sometimes you can feel that you're 'full', you're at capacity, you can't think any more – it's all a bit too much. If there are a lot of ideas going on in your head, then you need to start getting them out of there and stop thinking about them. Keep a checklist of things you need to do, so they're not on your mind. If you're thinking about what could happen in the future, don't let it take over your mind, you'll only do more damage. Spend time and talk to someone, find that outlet, as bottling things up inside is only going to cause you health issues – which   may be long term, so don't keep it all in – talk!

Health and nutrition is something that a busy schedule can leave behind, but it's the most important thing we need to maintain. Feed your body with healthy nutrition and your mind and body will be thankful. Then you will be able to keep that focus and productivity lasting when you need it. It's easy to fall into the trap of not finding time to eat, when the truth is, you're not making time to eat. You need to ensure that you are looking after the foundation of you!

Remind yourself of the freedom that you have in your own mind. You can visualise anything you want to, there's nobody stopping your freedom or getting in the way of it. If you want to be on the beach – close your eyes, think of the beach, the sun, the sea, the sand, the palm trees and take time out to enjoy your visualisation. If you can visualise this happening, then you are halfway there, you are preparing yourself for when you make that day happen! There is, however, a fine line between visualisation and getting your hopes up; don't try to make something look better than what it is, or what it could be. I'm a bit more pessimistic in that sense – I'll always play things down, so when it does happen it's even better, as opposed to being a little disappointed with the outcome.

So if you have that freedom in your mind, what's stopping you outside of your mind? Is it your surroundings? Circle of friends? Or is it just you?

Are you scared to fail? If so, why? What if failure is not an option? Do you remember when you were running so fast that you fell over? Or the first time you touched something so hot that it hurt? We only tend to get scared of things if we know what waits for us is the outcome of failure. So what is it that will makes you scared of failure?

You need to reflect and ask yourself a lot of these questions, and most of all – you need to be honest with yourself when answering them. Whether you make notes on paper, your computer, phone or as an exercise all in your head, do it and be honest. With those answers you've given, ask yourself why you've given that answer. You'll find that the more you dig the clearer it will become, and you will reach the point where you'll know what is holding back. Once you know what it is, it becomes easier to tackle.

If you are so scared of failure, why even think about doing something in the first place? Maybe you like the idea of it but you're too scared to develop it further? Why is that? Keep asking yourself these questions. You'll quickly narrow down to the answer.

Are you scared that you'll look like a fool and that some people may laugh at you? Well, you're not four years old anymore! Who cares! Those people who may laugh at you wouldn't be bringing you any good anyway. If you see a loved one fall over, the first human reaction is to help and ask, 'Are you OK?' Their fall and your thought process can both be so quick that by the time you've seen that they are OK, you start to laugh. But that doesn't mean you don't love them, that means you know they're not hurt, and they made a slight fool of themselves. Those people that will laugh at you when pain is real are the ones you shouldn't think about anyway, regardless of whether they are popular or successful. Keep those real ones around you close.

Everybody is scared of the unknown so that shouldn't stop you making the next moves you want to do to make it happen! If you're thinking, well, 2021 isn't looking good, what makes you think 2022 will be the best time to start that venture? The truth about starting anything is that there is never a great time or the perfect time to start. But you need to decide if you're really serious about doing it or if it just seems like a good idea. My take is that you're serious on doing it, but there is just that little bit of something that's keeping you away from running with it – find out what it is and deal with it! Now you know how you work best, when you work best and where you work best. Create a plan that's going to fit within a routine that you can stick to. There's no point in creating something that is unrealistic and you know won't last long – like that 5am wake up and run that seems to have taken over everyone's daily schedule. The change you implement doesn't have to be a radical change to your current way of working, but you do need to allocate time to what it is you need to achieve and stick to it, keep consistency, be repetitive and do what needs to be done until you're happy with the result.

You should support and encourage those around you, but don't focus on them, focus on you.

Don't focus on what others are doing, what others are wearing, where others are going – it's all completely irrelevant to you. Only you can make the best version of you. Your loved ones around you also care about you and I'm sure they want to support you, so keep them close. If things are getting tough and you seem to be closing off people from the outer circles, don't close off the ones that love and care for you – love and care for them back, too!

The bottom line in all of this is that you need to be true to yourself and you need to be the best version of you that's possible. Nobody is going to waltz over to you and do everything for you – that's all down to you. You take care of your appearance, your education, the way you conduct yourself in public, that's all you and your responsibility. These are things that you may or may not even be thinking about, but they all send a signal to others in the outside world.

Now there's part of me that always says 'You were born alone, and you'll die alone,' which can be seen as the sad truth or a pretty dark way to look at life. But I use this statement to push me forward, it says to me that you're alone. Every living individual has their own story – we all know what it's like to be alone and it's not nice, but in order to attract good people around you, you need to become that person, too. While people love you, only you know what's right for you and what your ambition in life is, or if you're not too sure yet, perhaps you have an idea of the direction you want to go and explore. Then go for it! What you don't want to become is unhappy, but even if you are unhappy now, you can change it – that's right, YOU!

Don't do what's expected of you, do what you would want to expect from yourself. Take pride in the tasks that you do, take pride in how well you keep yourself sharp and up-to-date on the topics that interest you, take pride in what you have achieved to date and take pride in what your future goals are. Be PROUD! You are alive, living and able to make a change, there is nothing stopping you from doing so – apart from YOU.

If you haven't quite found yourself but feel that you are shadowing someone – deal with it.

If you feel that you're going about your life as it's what's expected from you and you really want a change of career – change it!

If you have had a lifelong dream about exploring living in a foreign country or travelling the world and learning about culture – go for it!

If you've got a burning desire for that idea, opportunity or passion you have deep down inside to happen – make it happen! It takes guts to get out of your comfort zone; you know that you can do it, you're already thinking about the idea, so keep going with it and hopefully with a few tips from this book you can make it happen!

You do you, and let others do as they please – don't get distracted or obsessed with anyone else but yourself. if you learn to love yourself first, you will look after your physical and mental health. If you don't love yourself enough to look after yourself, how can you love others? Loving yourself isn't making 'look at me' statements or posting selfies with quotes. Loving yourself is taking care of your mental health and your physical health by nutrition and exercise. Learn to give your body the TLC it needs to repair and be ready for the exciting plans you have ahead.

Whatever it is that will make you happy, find it, embrace it, cherish it and make it happen!

18

Don't b*tch

Nobody wants to hear why things haven't gone to plan, or why things haven't worked out – especially if it's always someone or something else that's to blame. Then there becomes a common denominator in the mix which is you not making it happen. What tends to happen is when you start blaming things, talking behind people's back and generally bad mouthing, you start to build up this negativity around you. Look, everybody loves to hear some 'gossip', right, but there is a point when you cross the line of 'what you've heard / found out or has happened' that you then take it one step further and go out of your way to talk about this individual or entity.

The danger is that you keep on doing it, keep on not having anything nice to say. People will sense it, believe me, and they'll find it hard to talk to you, because all you'll end up doing is pushing negative comments about pretty much any topic they discuss. This habit has to be one of the worst traits you could have. If you find yourself doing it, stop.

Imagine you're with a potential client and both start bad mouthing a certain company or individual. Regardless of whether the client was the first one to 'start it', the fact that you've entertained that topic makes it just as bad. The outcome of this will be that you've demonstrated that you're willing to talk bad behind someone's back. Now, if you can do it about someone else with them, what's going to make them think that you won't talk about them to someone else? You've just clearly displayed you can do it! If this situation arises and for whatever reason you feel that you have to have your say, then don't entertain b*tch-ing about it. Instead, analyse the problem and give constructive criticism or your view on the situation in a professional tone. Don't degrade the company or individual and don't entertain anything that may be personal. The truth behind it all is, you don't know what demons they have going on in their own mind. They could be in a bad place and not know how to deal with it, among a million other things.

Shit happens; people fall ill as a reaction to stress, they divorce, they turn to drugs, alcohol, they do things that they shouldn't – most of these things can be prevented, but there is a cry for help early on that if you are close to that person, you can help. You can help not by feeding an addiction that's about to start, but by talking. Of course, there's a stage where you feel that you can't help because the advice is falling onto deaf ears or because it's a problem that's spiralling out of control; then you've got to get the professionals in to try to better things. I'm fortunate I've never had these problems, but I've lost people close to me that have – it's brutal, but you need to try to motivate them so they can pull themselves out of the problem they've fallen into. The worry is that you care for them only to find out they're abusing whatever it is behind your back. It's a really difficult situation, and after experiencing it from a close friend and seeing the knock-on effects, it can open your eyes even more to the dangers of falling into stress or trying to live up to expectations. But the message here is not to badmouth or b*tch – that energy you're using up could be used to help them out – give them a call and see how they're doing!

If something isn't going to plan, because of things out of your control like COVID-19, it means you can't operate.

Don't b*tch about it – change – adapt – succeed! If you've failed business after business.

Don't b*tch about it – keep on going, you will make it happen! If your relative or friend is doing well.

Don't b*tch about it – support them!

If you've just been taken for a ride because you made a bad judgement, don't b*tch about it – forget it and move on!

Whatever the external factor may be, you're not going to progress by sitting and moaning about it. You're only wasting time and energy on the subject, when you should be learning from whatever it is that's just happened. If you made a bet that team 'x' would beat team 'y' – but somehow team 'y' cheated and won – b*tch-ing won't change the outcome. The bottom line is that you lost the bet.

Let's not forget, we are a nation of moaners – it's what we do, more than any other nation! We moan, we love to moan about the weather, about the TV shows, about the fact that someone has just spilt a drop of tea on your new carpet. Whatever it is, you can be sure that we'll moan about it. It's just something we've grown up around, so it's almost embedded into our DNA.

Moaning is different to b*tch-ing!

Having a moan is good; you're sharing your views on why you're not happy with something and how you'd like to see it put right. It's not causing any harm to anyone and you're not going into any harmful detail that could offend someone personally.

B*tch-ing about something or someone is when you are deliberately putting them down, making a personal attack to the individual or entity and being immoral by spreading hate.

The big difference between the two is that you are either giving your point of view from having a moan or you are spreading hate.

You've seen all the social media posts, 'haters can hate', 'haters this', 'haters that'. What's it all about? Who cares? Why spend your time talking about irrelevant people? Why even give them space and a spotlight?

Can you imagine owning a clothing brand and wanting to create a partnership/endorsement with a celebrity, but for whatever reason, it doesn't work out. Do you run to social media and shout that that celebrity is a hater and they're hating on your brand? No – of course you don't!

What about the ice cream man, when you go to him and ask to buy a 50p ice cream cone and he tries to upsell you a £1 flake and you say no… does he drive away with his finger up to you shouting 'hater'?

Of course he doesn't – he might grumble a bit and have a moan but keeps it all good!

It's just silly! Don't fall into this trap of 'hating' or even entertaining it.

If someone doesn't like what you're doing – who cares!

Don't worry about pleasing everybody, but equally don't go out of your way to piss off those that are pleased with you. Doesn't everything flow smoother when people are happy? Sure it does, so try to keep a positive vibe about everything.

We all need positivity – it's been so easy to fall into this trap I've been talking about – b*tch-ing even much more so last year. In 2020 – stuck indoors, life on hold, global pandemic – so many took to social media platforms to moan and spoke to their closest ones about it. A lot of unfortunate things have happened too from job losses to marriage breakdowns. It's all breeding a lot of negativity and people are falling out with each other. I think this is not for the right reasons but out of a lot of frustration that has been building up over the last year.

Good friends, family, colleagues are voicing their views on several subjects from politics to the pandemic, which others don't like, and they're parting ways. Not good. Let's not divide ourselves by the views we have. Prior to the pandemic, it was easier because life was 'normal' – now when the world has stopped, these things tend to piss us off if we don't like them. When you see 'Billy' slating your favourite football team, it might hurt a bit more than normal, because we're all living with a bit more stress. But when 'Billy' starts telling you that the virus is fake, don't wear a mask and a loved one of yours has just died because of the virus, things tend to take a turn of direction. Now, what I do is respect everybody's point of view, that's their right. If they want to voice their opinion, then fine,. But if it becomes a message of hate or misinformation that can harm others, then that's where I draw the line. You shouldn't enter a confrontation with these people; fighting fire with fire never works. Perhaps you can reach out and see how they're doing, but it may lead to an information overload that you're not ready for and could cause a big argument that would end in both of you feeling sad.

If it's on social media and it's clogging up my timeline, I click 'hide' – simple. There's no need to lose a friend who's going through a tough time and probably dealing with it in this way. However, in the same way, I don't push my thoughts or views on anybody. People should be more respectful and do the same. I think in the hope that once we come out the other end of this and things get back to 'normal' that tensions will settle, and we'll all be a little happier like we used to be. Well, that's what I hope for.

Be gentle – everybody is a little broken, a little more fragile than they used to be, so remember to be nice. It costs nothing and will make that conversation or negotiation a little easier. A simple question the next time you talk to anybody next, ask them genuinely, 'Are you OK?' when you ask a genuine question like that, it hold a lot more weight than the 'You OK' line you automatically use on the phone. Take some time out to ask them the most important question of all.

The worry out of all of what's been going on recently is that the amount of b*tch-ing has turned into hate. Remember, if you fall out with everybody, you are left with nobody. Don't close the world off. If you start feeling a little more fragile than before, talk. Talk to your partner, your family, your friends, let them know how you are feeling. There's nothing wrong with sharing your emotion – it doesn't make you any weaker – in fact, it makes you a bigger person because you can confront a problem and talk about it. The more you chip away to find out why you're feeling the way you are – the sooner you have a clear answer. When it comes to emotion, you should speak out and talk to someone, as verbalising your feelings will hold a lot more weight than talking to yourself or thinking it through. When you express yourself through speech, you will find that you awaken your emotions, and your senses become alive. That's because you've probably not been talking about the real emotions you have inside, and your body needs to hear it.

We all have emotion – some wear it on their sleeve and some have it so hidden that you'll probably strike oil before you reach it. But as humans we go through a lot of emotional pain over time and it stays with us. Confront your emotions and spend time on them. Most of all, share the emotions with the ones you love. You'll feel better by sharing what you've been bottling up for a long time. It's a process but one you should practise.

Life is too short to b*tch and spread hate. You have to value your time and realise that you've got more important things to do than to talk about others. Keep your focus on what you want to achieve, that what's important is your direction and where you are going.

Don't worry about what anyone else is doing and most of all, don't b*tch!

Do it!

The most important part of all is the green light, the whistle blow, the gunshot to start the race. It's time to GO! Without doubt, it is the most exciting part of making things happen! Although, you might find out when you get going that it's not a straight race to the finish, but a bit like 'Supermarket Sweep' in the sense that you go forwards, backwards, turn around, and you're all over the place. But that doesn't matter, you're going! You're moving! There's nothing now holding you back and stopping you from doing what you want to do.

All of the effort you've put in for the big day is a bit like a marathon – you've trained, prepared, and know the plan of what speed you should keep per kilometre. All of the thought and preparation has gone into it and now it needs action. You've got that all-important plan that you can refer back to whenever you may need to, and you know what you're getting yourself in for.

Well, at least you think you do! But you're about to now make this whole thing come alive and go for it!

You may find that you hit the ground running and get to the finish line without any issues, or you may find some potholes on the way and you may trip and slip. But get back up and keep going – the main thing is that you're running with it. Imagine a relay race with the baton – well, that baton is your business plan with all the effort you've put into making it achievable. You've got it in your hand and you're running with it! Don't look back, don't drop the baton and finish the race!

This is now the point where you don't have to 'think' as much as before but now you just 'do it' – sounds easy right? Well it is! Especially if you've done all the groundwork. You are as prepared now as you will be. Don't try to put things off so you can 'do it' later, if you've set a target, 'do it'. Even if you've managed to talk your way right up until this point, you'll need to 'do it' – there's no way of getting out of it.

Now you separate the winners from the losers. Losers are those that talk a good talk – they may have even joined you on the journey right up until this point, talking their way through it. But now it's time to 'do it' and you'll see a clear difference between those that are doing things and those that are sitting back talking about things. Should you care? No. You've put in the effort and you know where you're going. Get out there and go!

Don't forget you've got those that have also come as far as you and they 'do it' too – maybe they're still doing it, but maybe you can do it better? How do you set yourself apart from someone similar? Why not just let them do it instead of you?

How many times have you looked at something and thought, 'I can do that' – then you give it a try and think 'Oh, actually it's not as easy as I thought it would be'. But if you keep at it, with practice you will get better and if you still believe you can do a better job, then why not?

A lot of businesses don't re-invent the wheel – they look at people in the market, they look at what they're offering and think, 'How can I make this better?' Maybe you've had a bad experience using a service that's made you think in this way, maybe you run a business that could branch out to offer that service or maybe you're just a maverick pioneer, who knows? But if you spot an opportunity and put in the effort, then what's stopping you from making it happen and making it better than what's already out there?

Probably the best example of this is Amazon. eBay was founded in 1995, but in 1996 Amazon was born. Yes, they just specialised in books to start with, but when they looked at the landscape to see what it was that they could improve, they went for it. Fast forward to 2021 and at the time of writing this, eBay's share price is circa $50 and Amazon's share price is circa $3,000 – need I say more? That's not the only example either. Look into companies like Index, Blockbuster and Toys

R Us, just to name a few. Their downfall was that they didn't move with the times. If you're not capturing the new upcoming generation of customers before they fall into your target, you'll lose them – it's that simple. In a fast-paced marketplace you need to be current – there are not many businesses making a profit by being from a past time that everyone would like to visit. There are a few of these, but they are not making that much – which then doesn't become a business, but more of a lifestyle.

So that may mean what you are ready to launch is something that those outside your generation bracket may not understand. Don't let that put you off – I have had so many generation clashes when it comes to business from family and people in business, more than I care to remember. It's because things change, time moves on and some people tend to get stuck in their ways if they haven't got their ear to the ground.

Always keep your ear to the ground – every tech company is trying to learn more and more about what trends are popular across various demographics. Everybody wants to know what you'll spend money on, so that they can make it for you – right? If you can keep your ear to the ground because you have a large network or you spend time with a lot of similar people to you, then you have an advantage of knowing what is current and what people are interested in. Already you're winning, and you probably don't even realise it.

If you are able to have a mentor, I'd suggest getting one. Having someone who can just spend some time to talk through things and give you their advice is worth so much. Don't think that having a mentor means that they'll do all the work for you, because they won't. If they did, you wouldn't learn anything and why would they drop everything they've got so as to make your passion work? Mentors are people who have set up successful businesses and organisations and have a track record of achievement. Now, don't think that you have to find the next Elon Musk to help you, but if you have anyone who you feel could help you, ask them. Be prepared to hear some things you might not want to hear like scrutiny. That's not putting you down, that's testing whether you really can handle it or make it work and above all to make sure there is a business there. It's important that you take your mentor's advice on board, but you don't necessarily need to take all of their advice as gospel – if that makes sense! But be respectful as they're taking time out to give advice. If you can learn from someone who's made it or has tried to make it work and failed then you're already a step ahead of them than they were when they started out. The more concise information that you can collect in order to be able to create a better judgement of decision – get it!

Whatever I've put my mind to in the past I've managed to achieve it, in some way, shape or form. We are all human and we are capable of making things happen! Never think to yourself, oh I could never do that. Why couldn't you? Nothing makes anyone far more superior than anybody else. We are all equal but different, different in what we choose to spend our time on, what we choose to spend our efforts on and where we choose to place our energy. It's energy that you can put into anything to achieve results.

Nothing is impossible. If you have a passion for something – do it!

If you want to start a side hustle – do it! someone tells you that you can't make it happen – do it!

It seems like everything in the world is going against you – do it! If you're the only person stopping yourself from doing it – do it! Keep pushing yourself, keep going and do it!

There is no 'right way' of making things happen! You've got to have the fundamentals in place in terms of your own development, you've got to be savvy, educated in the sector of interest and if you aren't – get learning about it and, all importantly, take that risk. There is always an element of risk within everything. Even now when you're at this point, something can happen that will risk your venture being a success, but maybe you've even managed to foresee that problem so you can prevent it from happening. Perhaps the path and plan changes from what was initially planned; so what? If your plan was to enter the water and you entered it, but you found a nicer spot in the water somewhere else, go to it – why not? Don't be afraid to change track; only be afraid if you're standing still. Keep moving and keep going!

You'll notice throughout the whole of the book that I haven't focused the narrative about money; money should never be the reason for you to fulfil your passion. What you need to focus on is what will make you happy. Sure, money will make you happy for short periods of time, but do you know how many people out there have money and are not happy? A lot more than you think! Everybody thinks about that lottery win, millions falling from the sky out of nowhere and into your bank account. But what will you do with it? What will keep you occupied? Think of all those doctors and nurses battling every day to save lives throughout the pandemic. They've found their passion, their calling, and they love what they do. That's something you cannot put a price on, that humanity that they are risking their own lives to save ours. The fact that they go into 'work' to save lives should say it all. Remember that we all come into this world with no material possessions and when we go we don't take them with us either.

I'll never forget having a meal in Moscow with a friend who is very successful in his art. We were in this wonderful place full of beautiful paintings, classical music, fine wine, great food and even better company. We were talking about Moscow as a city and the opportunities that it has for young people. But we were in a place where you could just smell money. Everything was pristine, from the food, drink, cigars – you name it. We were in London's Mayfair in the middle of Moscow. I turned to my friend and I said to him:

'After spending so much time here in Moscow, I still cannot believe how much money (wealth) there is around here.'

'Yes, Lazar ... but how to get it?!' he said.

We all burst out laughing immediately – my sides were sore from laughing for the rest of the evening. The thing is, my friend is hugely popular and very well respected, but he has passion for what he does and he has respect for what he does – there isn't a price that you can put on many things such as that. He's found his passion and the art he shares with the rest of the world is something that cannot be traded or bought. His answer to me is what everyone in the world is focused on – 'how to make money', 'financial freedom', in the hope that it will make their life better. His answer was a nod to those searching as money doesn't solve problems – it may only solve bills. To enjoy wealth is being content and passionate in what you do. If you can find what your passion is or make your idea something that can grow and other people will want to be part of, something that will also inspire them to be a great member of your team, then you're on the right road to be creating something that'll make a difference.

Life isn't about the material things and if you're not confident without having those material things, then maybe there's an issue to be addressed. We all like material things, sure, there are a lot of toys and nice things we like to have. But there is a big danger of becoming superficial with that and losing your true qualities if you will be judging someone on what they wear, or what they choose to show. Think about it – what's more powerful, somebody who has to prove something to you by being brash and flash with all that glitters, or somebody silent who could potentially buy everything you see, but they don't show you that card – they have no need. My view on this is don't fall into chasing money just for the numbers, but focus on your own venture/s, team/s and what you have going on and make it the best. Enjoy the rewards, but don't make them the sole reason for any venture, as you might be disappointed.

When someone says 'retirement' I think that's something I'll never be able to do. I'll just never be able to stop, because that is my passion, making things happen! I love to see new ideas come to life – there's nothing more exciting for me than bringing something to life from nothing. It's something that I'll continue to do for as long as I live – it's my passion!

But now it's all down to you, your passion, your hard work and your determination to make it happen!

DO IT!
MAKE IT HAPPEN!

ACKNOWLEDGEMENTS

This book began as most things do, an idea. I remember thinking one day, 'I would love to write a book.' Funnily enough, that one day was January 2020. I even found the note on my phone, but it was only the back end of 2020 that I decided to put it into action and get writing!

First and foremost, to my beautiful, loving and caring wife – Danica. Your honest opinion on everything I do is the opinion I pay the most attention to.

My children Konstantin and Jelica for keeping my inner child alive and always keeping me on my toes.

My parents. My father, Vido – we've had our differences over the years, but I have you to thank for my childhood memories and experiences. My late mother – Jelica (Helen) – a woman who was the most valuable asset in my life, who taught me how to be a gentleman and value others. A person I'd soon realise was like no other person I'd ever meet on this planet.

My uncle Radovan, who has always been there for me in life, no matter what – like the brother I never had.

My uncle Sava who first taught me how to aim and makes sure I've always got my eye on target. My aunt Dragica for all her facetime calls throughout lockdown and her love!

My cousin Igor, who first introduced me to the Balkans and the ways of doing business over there. A truly inspiring person!

HRH Crown Prince Alexander and HRH Crown Princess Katherine of Serbia, alongside Patricia and Robert, for having faith in me to run Lifeline Humanitarian Organisation in the UK and for answering my emails and calls whenever I have 'another idea'.

John and Carol Challis for giving me the opportunity to enter a whole new world of entertainment and becoming friends for life. Your determination, consistency and work ethic are things that I hugely admire.

James Collier, my closest friend (by distance). Although your jokes are not as good as mine, the ability you have as a visionary is much better. A true 'wise man'.

Nick Jones for editing this book to make it comprehensible in such a short space of time.

Stanislav Kruhliak for getting design on point and working around the clock as always!

Tom Ireland for staying awake during the hours of recording time in the studio making this audio book come alive.

The many business-minded people I enjoy spending time with to mull over ideas, concepts, plans – especially Jovica, Rade and Jignesh.

To many of you that I may have referred to in the book but not mentioned by name. You all know who you are – thank you!

Also, to all those I have ever done any business with – any discussions, deals or even fallouts – they've only made me better!

Not to forget my sisters and cousin without whom I wouldn't be an expert bride seller!

To all of you who have purchased this book and taken time out to read it or listen to it reach out, let me know your thoughts or beg me never to write a book again!

THANK YOU!